Kitchens

A *Sunset* Design Guide

by Karen Templer and the editors of *Sunset,* with Sarah Lynch

Contents

Over the past couple of decades, we have collectively come to terms with the fact that the kitchen is where the action is. We live in our kitchens, whether we mean to or not, and it's changed our expectations. Now, rather than trying to figure out how to keep backpacks and party guests out of the kitchen, we want a space that welcomes all comers, and handles them gracefully. Rather than running to the office computer to look up a recipe or to the laundry room to switch loads, we want to manage the household's affairs from command central: the modern kitchen.

Whether you're creating a new kitchen or improving your old one, the trick is to tailor it to the way *you* live. We're here to help. Armed with the photos, information, and expert advice found here, you're sure to design a kitchen that not only makes the most of your space and your funds but improves your quality of life.

ISBN-13: 978-0-376-01437-5
ISBN-10: 0-376-01437-7
Library of Congress Control
Number: 2013930384

Second Edition. First Printing 2013
Printed in the United States of America

OXMOOR HOUSE, INC.
Editorial Director: Leah McLaughlin
Creative Director: Felicity Keane
Brand Manager: Fonda Hitchcock
Managing Editor: Rebecca Benton

TIME HOME ENTERTAINMENT INC.
Publisher: Jim Childs
VP, Brand and Digital Strategy:
Steven Sandonato
Executive Director, Marketing Services:
Carol Pittard
Executive Director, Retail & Special Sales:
Tom Mifsud
*Director, Bookazine Development and
Marketing:* Laura Adam
Executive Publishing Director: Joy Butts
Associate Publishing Director:
Megan Pearlman
Finance Director: Glenn Buonocore
Associate General Counsel: Helen Wan

SUNSET PUBLISHING
President: Barb Newton
Editor-in-Chief: Peggy Northrop

CONTRIBUTORS TO THIS BOOK
Managing Editor: Bridget Biscotti Bradley
Photo Editor: Philippine Scali
Production Manager: Linda M. Bouchard
Photo Coordinator: Danielle Johnson
Imaging Specialist: Kimberley Navabpour
Project Editor: Lacie Pinyan
Proofreader: John Edmonds
Indexer: Marjorie Joy
Series Designer: Vasken Guiragossian

To order additional publications,
call 1-800-765-6400

For more books to enrich your life,
visit **oxmoorhouse.com**

Visit Sunset online at **sunset.com**

For the most comprehensive selection
of Sunset books, visit **sunsetbooks.com**

For more exciting home and garden ideas,
visit **myhomeideas.com**

Design Panel

The following design and building professionals from across the United States lent their enormous talent and valuable advice to the pages of this book.

Erik Barr
DESIGN PRINCIPAL

With a background in carpentry and construction, a degree in architecture, and experience in large and small firms on both coasts, Erik Barr set up shop as Urban Wedge, LLC, in Seattle. The small firm specializes in additions, remodels, and furniture design, taking a green building approach. Erik's renovated condominium was recently featured in *Sunset* magazine.
urbanwedge.com | *See Erik's Seattle kitchen on pages 140–143.*

Martha Angus
INTERIOR DESIGNER

Martha Angus is the principal of her own design firm, with offices in New York and San Francisco. A self-described "painter at heart," she studied at the École des Beaux Arts, Carnegie Mellon University, and Sotheby's Restoration, and brings a fine-arts approach to her interior design projects. Her work has been featured in *Elle Decor, The New York Times, Architectural Digest,* Australia's *Vogue Living,* and more.
marthaangus.com | *See a "sturdy" yet elegant kitchen–family room by Martha on pages 196–199.*

Kevin Price
ARCHITECT

Kevin Price grew up in Boulder and attended the University of Colorado, and it was Colorado that shaped his respect for the environment and his design approach. He has worked at Seattle's J.A.S. Design Build for more than a decade. A full-service company, J.A.S. has been building homes and communities through inspired design and thoughtful craft for more than 15 years. Kevin's work is featured regularly in *Sunset* magazine.
jasdesignbuild.com | *See Kevin's reinterpretation of a Craftsman kitchen on pages 52–53.*

Michelle Rein
ARCHITECTURAL DESIGN

Northern California natives Michelle Rein and her partner, Ariel Snyders, created American Artisans. The San Carlos, California, company unites their backgrounds in architectural design and fabrication. The duo designs one-of-a-kind interiors that feature their fine cabinetry, furniture, and architectural glass along with the work of other highly skilled artisans working in steel, stone, and hand-applied finishes.
amartisans.com | *See Michelle's work in the dramatic kitchen on pages 116–119.*

Neal Schwartz
ARCHITECT

Neal Schwartz holds dual master's degrees in architecture and public policy from Harvard. He is currently an associate professor at California College of the Arts; the principal of his own San Francisco architectural firm, Schwartz and Architecture; and a director on the board of the National AIDS Memorial Grove. His work has been featured in *Dwell, Western Interiors,* and *Sunset,* among other publications. **schwartzandarchitecture.com** | *See Neal's modernization of a San Francisco Victorian on pages 48–51 and his own kitchen on pages 96–99.*

Brian Eby
CABINETMAKER/GENERAL CONTRACTOR

Brian Eby is the principal of Eby Construction, Inc., a full-service Bay Area design build company. He has been in the building trades since childhood, when he "helped" his father with weekend projects. After several years as a cabinetmaker and carpenter, he transitioned into construction management, staying involved in the hands-on work while also enjoying a role in design and planning. His work has appeared in *The New York Times.* **visiteby.com** | *See Brian's renovation of a historic residence's kitchen on pages 170–173.*

Bill Ingram
ARCHITECT

After graduating from Auburn University with a degree in architecture in 1983, Bill Ingram settled in Birmingham, where he runs a private firm designing houses throughout the Southeast, as well as around the country. His work has been featured in *Southern Accents, House and Garden, Veranda, House Beautiful,* and *Cottage Living.* **billingramarchitect.com** | *See Bill's own Alabama kitchen on pages 136–139.*

Benjamin Nutter
ARCHITECT

Benjamin Nutter, AIA, has practiced residential and commercial architecture for over 30 years. A graduate of the University of Oregon, Ben trained under Royal Barry Wills before opening an office in his Massachusetts hometown, in 1984. A committed volunteer and advocate of regionally inspired and environmentally sensitive design, he is a past chairman of the Topsfield Building Committee and stewarded an award-winning renovation of the Topsfield Town Hall. His work appears in several books as well as *This Old House, New Old House,* and *Yankee* magazines. **benjaminnutter.com** | *See Ben's work in a home originally built in 1720 on pages 92–95.*

Kathryn Rogers
ARCHITECT

Kathryn Rogers is the founder of Sogno Design Group, which focuses on residential design in the San Francisco area. She has a degree in architecture from Virginia Polytechnic and a background in historic preservation and restoration. She was a board member of Architects, Designers, and Planners for Social Responsibility (ADPSR) for 10 years and continues to incorporate green building methods in her projects. **sognodesigngroup.com** | *See a family-friendly kitchen by Kathryn on pages 144–147.*

Bobby McAlpine
ARCHITECT

Alabama architect Bobby McAlpine designed his first house at the age of 5 and hasn't stopped since. In addition to his architecture and interior design firm, McAlpine Tankersley, he has a prominent line of furniture for Lee Industries. His work has been featured in *Southern Accents, House Beautiful, Cottage Living,* and many other national, regional, and international publications. **mcalpinetankersley.com** | *See a Zen-like beach house kitchen by Bobby on pages 72–75.*

Kathy Farley
INTERIOR DESIGNER

Kathy Farley's Albany, California, company Artdecor specializes in creative, modern design concepts for residential and commercial projects. With her fine-arts background and her extensive work in the field of color, she has established a studio recognized for its eclectic design and color approach. Her home has been featured in *Sunset.* **artdecorhome.com** | *See Kathy's own colorful kitchen on pages 174–177.*

Chapter 1

Getting Started

Cabinetry, counters, flooring, appliances—designing a kitchen involves a raft of choices. But before all of the details can be decided, there are more basic questions: What kind of kitchen will suit your needs? Will it require a simple facelift or an extensive remodel? How much space and how much money are available? Will you do any of the work yourself? Whatever the type and scale of your project, organizing your ideas accordingly will allow you to make smart decisions along the way.

An all-white kitchen is the perfect choice for a remodel because it will never go out of style. The dark-stained wood floors, marble slab counters, and stainless-steel appliances are current favorites in kitchen trends, but the overall look still feels classic and timeless.

Investing Wisely

A kitchen is an investment, with impact on both your quality of life and the value of your house. You want to create a space that fulfills your wishes without losing sight of resale issues. Often, a house will change hands before a kitchen remodel has become outdated, so it's important to keep in mind "the context of your local real estate market," as contractor Brian Eby says, "and not just your own personal taste."

The Value of a Dream Kitchen

Ask 10 people to describe the perfect kitchen and you're likely to get 10 very different answers. One person might want an open space suitable for entertaining, while another prefers a contained kitchen so that nobody sees dirty dishes from the family room. One person might cook rarely and choose basic appliances, while another would settle for nothing less than a professional-grade range. One might create a kitchen like her grandmother's, with an apron sink and checkerboard floor. Yet another would craft a modern space in steel and glass.

The first step in creating your dream kitchen, of course, is to figure out your must-haves and your would-be-nice lists. For starters, ask yourself how you use your current kitchen—which aspects of it suit you and which frustrate you. You might love the layout of your kitchen but long for a hardwood floor and a gas range. Or it might be that your fridge is too far from your sink, your appliance doors bang into each other, and you don't have the counter space for the baking projects you love. Noting real-world shortcomings can be as helpful as making wish lists, so be sure to do both. As you begin to weigh all the elements, think in terms of longevity and make choices—both of style and function—that will suit your household's evolving needs as the years go by. That way your kitchen will have lasting value.

ABOVE This new kitchen's combination of white cabinets, bamboo-topped island, and gray floors and backsplash creates a neutral backdrop that gives the owners carte blanche for their own style, as well as resale value for the future.

OPPOSITE PAGE This farmhouse-style kitchen capitalizes on a vaulted ceiling and floor space that allows for a central table, which can be used as a prep area when needed.

Market Value

As you zero in on your personal ideals, weigh them against the matter of property value. It's often said that "kitchens sell houses," and regardless of whether you intend to sell in the near term, you want to make improvements that are commensurate with expectations and property values in your area, avoiding either underimproving or overimproving. Contractor Brian Eby recommends soliciting input from savvy realtors. "They'll have seen a lot of kitchens and will know what buyers are looking for in your area. They're likely to advise something that's a value-add that you'd never have thought of."

To underimprove would be to exclude things that aren't important to you but could be to the next owner. Wood flooring might be all the rage in your neighborhood, for example, while not a priority for you. But if your home goes on the market with vinyl flooring and two homes similar to yours are for sale with wood, it could be a sticking point.

On the other hand, comparative home prices might be such that it would be unlikely you could recoup the cost of marble counters, so investing in them would be overimproving. Even if you decide that something is important to you—and you intend to stay in your home long enough—that the financial return on your investment isn't an issue, you still want to make informed decisions, especially on the big-ticket items.

OPPOSITE PAGE In a multi-unit building like this one converted from an old warehouse, upgrading the kitchen with top-of-the-line appliances and stainless counters increases the real estate value and helps set the unit apart from others in the building.

RIGHT This compact kitchen was remodeled for someone who loves to cook, but the expense of the six-burner professional range, twin sinks, and dishwasher drawers risks overimprovement when it comes to resale value.

Assessing the Project

This space was gutted and given a total makeover within the footprint of the former kitchen (inset). The passageway to the back door was narrowed to make more room for cabinets and the refrigerator. The front wall of the space was flattened, the opening widened, and a door on a barn rail added. The door adds character in addition to acting as a room divider when needed.

BEFORE

Remodeling a kitchen poses a different set of challenges than creating a new kitchen from scratch. Whether your remodel will be moderate or major depends largely on your budget but also on the structural state of your current kitchen and how far it is from meeting your functional and aesthetic objectives.

Moderate Makeover

Freshening up your personal appearance can be simple or dramatic, considering that your choices range from a wardrobe update to a haircut to plastic surgery. In the same way, if you have a small

budget or your kitchen already meets its primary functions, you may choose to make only cosmetic changes. At the easy and inexpensive end of the continuum is a fresh coat of paint on the walls and cabinets. Replacing outdated appliances—or even the sink—can also greatly change the look of things while providing a functional upgrade. For a slightly larger project, you can consider installing new flooring or counters or retiling a backsplash. If your cabinets are good and sturdy but you dislike the look of them, you can go beyond changing the paint or hardware to replacing the doors with something more to your liking. A combination of these options can result in a kitchen that's entirely new and different, without the cost of more elaborate measures.

Full or Partial Renovation

The advantage of a renovation is that it allows you to address issues of layout and appliance placement as well as

update the style. Once you start moving things around within the space of the kitchen—whether it's a wall or a stove—you're into the realm of renovation, which means a more time-consuming and costly undertaking.

Removing (or halving) a non-load-bearing wall can be a relatively simple operation. Relocating appliances can be somewhat more involved. Anything that requires venting, plumbing, gas, or electricity will require the services of a professional, or at least a very skilled homeowner. Moving the stove, for instance, might mean installing another gas hookup and vent; moving or adding a sink would require new plumbing. And reconfiguring space almost always means new cabinets, which tend to be the biggest portion of any kitchen budget. If you're planning a renovation—from removing a wall to shuffling the space—it's best to involve an architect or designer who can ensure you get the best kitchen for your money.

BEFORE

BEFORE

Major Overhaul

The most extensive type of kitchen makeover is one that involves adding or annexing space to enlarge the footprint of the kitchen. You might be surprised at how many ways there are to open up or reconfigure most kitchens within their existing space, but if you have a small galley kitchen and you want an island, a breakfast nook, and a home office, you'll need to either build an addition or take over existing space, such as a porch, garage, or even part or all of an adjacent room. An addition obviously offers the most flexibility in accomplishing your goals, and the most dramatic change from "before" to "after." But along with labor and materials, you'll need to factor in the added fees and time necessary to obtain permits for the job. Be aware that any addition beyond a small bump-out will require a foundation and roof, and possibly changes to your existing roofline. It's best to hire an experienced architect who can design an addition that will integrate seamlessly with your home and create the most efficient kitchen in the added space.

Taking over space from a den and hallway allowed for a total reconfiguration of this kitchen without adding onto the house. A new island with seating on one side meant the kitchen door could be moved, a partial wall removed, and the counters extended into the formerly cramped eating nook, which now houses built-in bookshelves. The ceiling was opened up to include a skylight and new rafters. A small desk area was carved out of the end of the counter, where the fridge once was.

Creating Space

This loft's L-shaped kitchen shows how a culinary workstation can be carved out of any corner if you complete the work triangle with an island.

How well your kitchen functions depends as much on smart organization as it does on square footage. No matter how little room you have to work with, there are many ways to create openness and maximize functionality.

Layout Basics

A growing trend toward open, multifunctional kitchens has brought a new spaciousness to smaller kitchens and changed the conversation when it comes to traditional layouts like those at right. New homes with enclosed kitchens are increasingly rare, and older homes are being remodeled to open the kitchens up to ever-larger great rooms. Meanwhile, a trend toward home cooking and entertaining—and on kitchens designed for those activities—has led to a rise in built-in islands and modular appliances, all of which change the equation where layout is concerned.

The traditional layouts seen here are still pertinent, no matter how one might modify them, since the basic design tenets hold true. The guiding focus of kitchen design has always been the "work triangle"—created when you draw a line from the sink to the refrigerator to the stove and back to the sink. These are the zones most frequently used, so the triangle represents the most-traveled path. Ideas about the optimal distance between these key elements are debated and evolving, but keeping the three points of the triangle within reasonable proximity gets more critical as kitchens get more complex.

Work triangle aside, most designers have specific ideas about various aspects of layout. Architect Erik Barr, for instance, insists on a 5-foot minimum of uninterrupted countertop. "Two people can comfortably work next to each other at 5 feet." In a smaller kitchen—such as his own, seen on pages 140–143—that means pushing the appliances to the ends of the counter. He also steers clear of corner cabinets, sticking to straight runs of cabinetry. "So I avoid L's and U's and all the things that create oddball cabinet and counter spaces."

For designer Michelle Rein, the first priority is a 44-inch-wide aisle, "for good flow." She says, "Many people have smaller kitchens and want to stick as much stuff in there as possible. It causes traffic problems. Less than 44 inches looks uncomfortable and makes even a large kitchen seem smaller." But most designers agree that there are no strict rules. What works best for your kitchen will depend on the amount of space you have, the number of cooks, the number of appliances, and how you tend to work. Of course, some things never change: The dishwasher and trash (including compost bins and compactors) should always be by the sink, and the oven should have counter space nearby where hot dishes can rest.

SAMPLE KITCHEN LAYOUTS

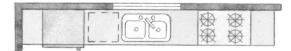

One wall

Galley (corridor)

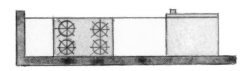

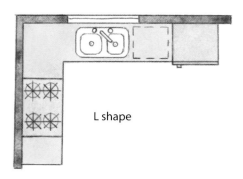

L shape

U shape

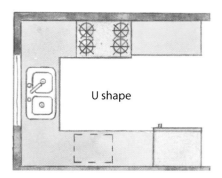

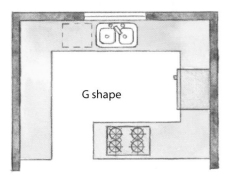

G shape

ABOVE There's plenty of room in this loft for a more elaborate kitchen, but with the formal living room around the corner, the designer-homeowner kept the kitchen to one wall and included a generous sectional where guests can lounge while he cooks, turning the kitchen into a true gathering space.

LEFT Adding cabinets to the second wall of this room would have made for cramped eating quarters, and the table was a higher priority. Stools are a smart choice in a small area, since they occupy little visual space and can be pushed all the way under the table if necessary.

The One-Wall Kitchen

The traditional one-wall kitchen is just that: a single bank of cabinets along one wall of a space, with a fridge, sink, and stove integrated into it (nearly always arranged with the sink in between the other two). It may be one wall of a studio apartment or loft, or it may be a dedicated kitchen so compact that it can hold cabinets and appliances on only one wall, leaving room for a table and chairs.

For people who don't cook often or elaborately, a one-wall kitchen can be sufficient —and certainly cuts down on costs. More common these days, though, is the combination of the classic one-wall with an island. The island helps define the kitchen and can double the storage and work surfaces. It can also accommodate some seating, resulting in what may feel like a vastly larger kitchen. The sink or the stove can also be moved to the island so that not all tasks require people to face the wall. With or without an island, one-wall kitchens should maximize vertical space for storage.

A large island can easily expand a one-wall kitchen. This one allows for bench seating and provides a sink with a better view for easier interaction with guests.

A peninsula divides this small U-shaped kitchen from the dining area. Luckily the walls above the sink and the stove have plenty of storage.

The Galley and Other Small Kitchens

The galley (or corridor) is considered by many people to be the most efficient form a kitchen can take. With two banks of cabinetry and appliances on parallel walls, close together, everything is within easy reach for the cook. Some galley kitchens have an eating area at one end or the other, which has the benefit of keeping diners out of the busy cook's way.

If you have a galley kitchen and you want it to be more connected to the living areas, look into removing the upper half of one wall. You'll lose many of your upper cabinets, but you'll gain a sense of spaciousness and the potential for a counter with seating on the opposite side. You can make up for the loss of storage by placing additional cabinets on the outside of the half wall.

ABOVE LEFT Limited upper cabinets, one long counter, an uninterrupted expanse of floor, and the repetition of chandeliers all combine to make this galley kitchen seem larger than its actual size.

ABOVE RIGHT Tucked into a nook in a tiny studio apartment, this kitchen is fully functional despite its lack of counter space. A scaled-down stove and mini-fridge fit under the counter so that the opposite wall could be used for storage rather than appliances.

OPPOSITE PAGE, TOP LEFT An L-shaped layout and an island are a powerful combination, particularly with the inclusion of full-height cabinetry along the short wall.

OPPOSITE PAGE, TOP RIGHT Custom cabinets faced in reclaimed wood are one way to create "the un-kitchen." Sculptural lighting and unique textures like the river-rock wall behind the stove are just a few of the unexpected details.

OPPOSITE PAGE, BOTTOM A midsize kitchen like this G-shaped example is the perfect opportunity to get rid of upper cabinets as advised by architect Neal Schwartz, who touts the benefits of windows instead of banks of cabinets.

ABOVE This kitchen utilizes two islands and one well-disguised wall of appliances to create a series of food prep and dining zones that are integrated into the indoor/outdoor living room.

Midsize Kitchens

L-shaped, U-shaped, G-shaped— kitchens that have cabinetry wrapping multiple walls have taken on new forms over recent decades, with peninsulas creating breakfast bars, islands floating in the middle of the room, or all but the perimeter walls torn out. The most popular kitchen layout seems to be the L-shaped with an island—with or without seating—which fits neatly into a corner of any open-plan space or great room.

Minimalist Kitchens

Also on the rise is what might be called the un-kitchen, where the more obvious kitchen elements (such as the refrigerator and upper cabinets) are downplayed or tucked out of sight and where the kitchen area is designed with the same sensibility as the living space it has merged with. The fridge may be slipped discreetly into the island in the form of drawers, or it may be located in an adjacent pantry, along with copious storage space and an extra sink, nearby but out of view.

Deluxe Kitchens

Today's kitchens take too many forms to name or diagram, but many are large enough to accommodate an island, a dinner table, an office nook, and sometimes even a laundry closet. The bigger the kitchen, and the more numerous its sinks and appliances and dueling functions, the more thought must go into the layout to ensure that it performs efficiently.

Think in terms of work zones or stations—sink, stove, and refrigerator in one area, perhaps a drinks fridge and snack cabinet in another, and a baking center in a third. And never underestimate the value of a second sink in a large space. Also think strategically regarding traffic flow. You don't want people to have to walk through the main cooking area to grab a drink or set the table.

ABOVE You can't beat the luxury of a built-in island that is big enough to double your counter space, anchor a pair of stylish pendant lights, and accommodate multiple seats as well as a second sink.

ABOVE A matched set of scaled-down islands is both more functional and less imposing than one large one might have been. Traffic flows easily around both islands. One holds a prep sink, while the other is an uninterrupted work surface.

RIGHT Sink, cooktop, refrigerator, and microwave are smartly arranged on one side of this sizable kitchen. The less-often-used ovens and warming drawer are on the opposite wall. A small desk station is easily accessed from either direction.

Organizing Your Thoughts

OPPOSITE PAGE
Energy-efficient
appliances, reclaimed
wood flooring, and
bamboo countertops
are among the earth-
friendly choices that
were made in design-
ing this bright and
beachy space.

RIGHT If you have a
spacious kitchen but
not a sizeable budget,
consider painting the
cabinets, upgrading
the flooring, and
adding an off-the-rack
island like this small
butcher block that
offers a central prep
area and extra storage.

From materials and finishes to social and environmental responsibilities, a kitchen remodel means much to consider—and keep track of.

Gather Ideas

As you look through this book, take in the various aspects of the many kitchens pictured and flag those that stand out, whether for layout, appliances, or style details. Make notes on what you like about each kitchen you flag—you'll almost certainly find enough ideas to help you solidify your wishes as well as communicate them to contractors and a designer, should you use one.

Also, start a project folder—digital or old-fashioned—that you can share. As your kitchen plan evolves, you'll amass paint swatches, appliance spec sheets, photos of lights, countertops, and other items that you'll want to reference. Keep the folder with you when you shop and meet with contractors—it will help you arrive at the optimal design for your new kitchen.

Weigh Additional Factors

Beyond matters of style and surfaces, the following may be considerations:

ECO-CONSCIOUSNESS Committing to a green approach will have a major influence on your project. In addition to choosing environmentally responsible materials like cork flooring and counters made of recycled content, you may opt to refinish your cabinets (using low- or

no-VOC paint) and refurbish a stove rather than starting fresh. These measures will limit how much you send to the landfill and how much new manufacturing—and long-distance shipping—is done on your behalf.

UNIVERSAL AND ACCESSIBLE DESIGN If anyone in your household is elderly or disabled, aim for such features as wider aisles and doorways, lower counters, mid-wall receptacles and switches, lever faucets, and pullout shelves and work surfaces.

DO-IT-YOURSELFABILITY If you're on a limited budget or simply enjoy home-improvement projects, give that fact precedence when making decisions. For example, a custom marble-slab back-splash is pricey and heavy and should be installed professionally, whereas marble tiles are much less expensive and moderately skilled homeowners can do the tiling themselves. In choosing between options, the DIY factor may tip the scale.

Kitchen Worksheet

Filling out this questionnaire will help you consolidate your thoughts on the various issues touched on in this chapter and detailed in those that follow. Photocopy it or write in pencil, because your ideas are likely to evolve. Although you may find that you can't afford everything your dream kitchen encompasses, having this wish list will help to prioritize your choices.

Getting Started (pages 6–27)

What's your primary motivation for changing your kitchen?

_____

What do you like about your current kitchen?

_____

What do you dislike about your current kitchen?

_____

How long do you expect to own your home?

_____

You cook/entertain ❑ often ❑ average ❑ rarely

Does your kitchen need to accommodate multiple cooks?
❑ yes ❑ no

You plan to ❑ change the size and/or layout
　　　　　　 ❑ make only cosmetic changes

Will you move or remove any walls, doors, or windows?

_____

Do you want to incorporate any additional functions?
❑ mudroom ❑ desk ❑ bar ❑ pet care/feeding
❑ laundry facilities ❑ other _____

Kitchen seating will be in the form of
❑ a peninsula or island counter
❑ a kitchen/dining table (to seat how many: ___)

Which professionals will the job require?
❑ plumber ❑ electrician ❑ tile layer or counter installer
❑ general contractor ❑ architect ❑ designer

Will you do any of the work yourself? _____

Are you concerned about ❑ environmental impact
　　　　　　　　　　　　 ❑ accessibility issues

Cabinets (pages 30–53)

Will you keep any existing cabinets? ❑ refinish/repaint
❑ replace hardware ❑ reface ❑ replace cabinets (some/all)

New cabinets will be:
❑ stock ❑ semi-custom ❑ custom ❑ face-frame ❑ frameless

What will the door style be?

_____

The desired finish is (indicate colors and placement if using multiple finishes):

❑ painted _____

❑ wood (light/dark) _____

❑ laminate _____

❑ stainless steel _____

❑ other _____

What kind of knobs and pulls?

_____

You want and have room for a:
❑ built-in island ❑ freestanding island ❑ peninsula

Counters and Backsplashes (pages 54–83)

Indicate counter material preferences for any areas that apply:
perimeter counters _____
peninsula _____
island _____

What edge style? _____

Do you want your counters to incorporate any extras?
❑ knife slots ❑ trash chute ❑ trivet strips ❑ drainboard

Your backsplash will be ❑ partial ❑ full wall

Of what material? _____

Sinks and Faucets *(pages 84–99)*

Indicate how many sinks and note which type (drop-in, undermount, integrated, apron) and material (enameled cast iron, ceramic, stone, steel, etc.) for each:

❑ primary _____

❑ prep _____

❑ other _____

Your primary sink will be ❑ single-basin ❑ multi-basin

Your primary faucet will be:
❑ center-set ❑ spread-fit ❑ exposed bridge
❑ counter-mounted ❑ wall-mounted

Indicate which of the following you will include and note any related preferences:

❑ sprayer _____

❑ purified water tap _____

❑ soap dispenser _____

❑ pot filler _____

Appliances *(pages 100–123)*

Check all appliances you intend to incorporate and write in preferences of style, size, and color or finish:

❑ refrigerator(s) _____

❑ wine fridge _____

❑ range _____

❑ cooktop _____

❑ hood/ventilation _____

❑ wall oven(s) _____

❑ microwave/other oven(s) _____

❑ warming drawer _____

❑ dishwasher _____

❑ trash compactor _____

❑ other _____

Flooring *(pages 124–147)*

You plan to ❑ keep your existing floor ❑ refinish it
❑ replace it

With what type of flooring? _____

In what pattern? _____

Storage and Display *(pages 148–181)*

Is there any existing pantry space? ❑ yes ❑ no

If yes, do you intend to ❑ preserve it ❑ demolish it?

If not, do you wish to add a pantry or pantries? ❑ yes ❑ no
If yes, what type? _____

Do you want a ❑ pot rack and/or ❑ plate rack?

You want built-in specialty storage for
❑ cookbooks ❑ small appliances ❑ wine ❑ spices
❑ collections of any sort

Finishing Touches *(pages 182–205)*

Note any needs and preferences with regard to the following:

❑ color _____

❑ wall treatment _____

❑ ceiling treatment _____

❑ windows _____

❑ window treatments _____

❑ lighting _____

❑ seating _____

❑ artwork _____

❑ other _____

Getting It Done *(pages 206–213)*

What is the timetable for completing the project?

_____

Which approvals and/or permits will you need?

_____

_____

What is your budget?

_____

Notes: _____

_____

_____

_____

_____

_____

_____

Chapter 2

Cabinets

Whether you're upgrading your cabinets or designing a kitchen from scratch, the number of available options has never been greater—from methods of case construction to the range of materials and offerings in specialty storage. Cabinets create the structural and stylistic base of the kitchen. That means decisions about how much cabinetry you will need, which type you would like, and what level of customization you can afford are not to be taken lightly.

This white kitchen with green accents features a combination of glass-fronted cabinet doors and solid-paneled doors. The range hood is styled to match the cabinetry.

Cabinet Considerations

A coat of paint can transform the look of kitchen cabinets. Here, doors were left off some of the uppers, and the upper and lower cabinets were painted two different colors to give the space a dynamic feel.

W hat sets one cabinet apart from another is not just the color and style but the materials and how the cases are faced and finished. Having a solid understanding of various cabinet styles and terminology will prepare you for a more detailed discussion with your retailer, designer, or cabinetmaker.

Refinish or Replace?

Cabinets are the most integral part of kitchen design, and they take up a big percentage of a renovation budget—approximately 50 percent. Start off by assessing your storage needs and the possibility of incorporating your existing cabinets into your dream kitchen.

First determine the quality and condition of your cabinets: Are the doors scratched or damaged? Are the shelves and door hinges sturdy? Next, you'll want to consider the style factor; if you're dreaming of a country kitchen and your cabinets are faced with laminate, you may decide to start shopping for new cabinets. But before making a decision, assess your storage needs. Determine how much space you will require—don't forget to note the dimensions of your widest plates and tallest glasses—and compare it with that of your existing cabinets. If your cabinets are in good condition and they meet your storage needs, consider refinishing or refacing them.

Refinishing is the easiest and most cost-effective way to change the look of your cabinets. Picture your outdated wooden cabinets sanded and given a fresh coat of glossy white paint or a richer stain. Refinishing your cabinets could be a relatively simple weekend DIY project or a quick job for a local painter. Factor in new knobs and pulls, and you could effect a total transformation.

Refacing—or swapping out the doors—is the next level of defense against unsightly kitchen cabinets. A kitchen can look outdated because of the style and material of the cabinet doors, timeworn from years of daily use. The numerous options for stock door replacements offer a chance to change both the color and the overall style of your kitchen for a fraction of the cost of a total overhaul. Even the drawers, which might have old wooden rails they don't quite slide on, can be replaced with new ones on modern glides.

However, there are situations in which keeping your old cabinets might actually cost you more than buying new ones. "Resurrecting something can take a lot more effort than it does to start fresh," says architect Kevin Price. For instance, older cabinets with holes for built-in appliances might not accommodate newer equipment. The additional planning and troubleshooting can require a lot of your designer's and contractor's time, and time equals money.

TOP Well-built cabinets, like the ones in this old-fashioned country kitchen, can last through many renovations if you're prepared to refinish them when they start to look worn.

BOTTOM Bookmatched walnut veneers were used to reface the cabinets in this small kitchen. The result is rich and warm yet thoroughly contemporary.

Finding Your Style

It can be overwhelming to try to envision your dream kitchen. You may know that you like white paneled cabinets and love the look of marble. But when you're faced with a showroom full of white door samples and dozens of 3-inch stone squares, all your convictions may be lost. Nailing down the design of your cabinet doors can be a great starting point.

The options range from thin slabs of man-made material to multi-paned wooden doors inset with chicken wire, and chances are you aren't interested in the entire spectrum. If your style is modern, begin by looking at simple plain-front doors and then consider some of the edgier European looks or natural textured options. If you know you want something more traditional, determine whether you want your kitchen to feel formal or rustic. If it's elegance you're leaning toward, focus on the shapes of paneled wooden doors. For a vintage feel, consider framed glass doors or Cape Cod–style beadboard. Once you narrow down the selection, you will easily be able to find a cabinet style that suits your home.

Another choice you'll want to consider early on is whether you want your cabinets traditionally "fitted" or whether you want to go for a more European "unfitted" look, which has a mix of finishes and a different approach to upper cabinets. The standard modern American kitchen has banks of upper and lower cabinets spanning the walls, with the sink and appliances built into them as in a ship's galley. But that's not your only option. Built-in cabinets can be replaced with freestanding storage furniture, and upper cabinets may take on traditional hutch styling, sitting right on the counter rather than floating above it. More and more, uppers are disappearing entirely or being replaced by open shelving or plate racks.

ARCHITECT
NEAL SCHWARTZ ON

Upper Cabinets

Uppers start to encroach on the feeling of space," says Schwartz, who prefers not to include them in a kitchen and compensates for the lost storage by including a full-height pantry cabinet. When he does use uppers, he runs them all the way to the ceiling "so that they feel like they're part of the wall rather than boxes hanging off the walls."

ABOVE LEFT For a style that is all your own, try combining various textures and materials you like. This playful yet sophisticated kitchen includes chicken wire insets, a stainless-steel backsplash, painted wooden cabinets, and a granite countertop.

OPPOSITE PAGE, TOP Slab-style horizontal cabinet doors set the tone for a contemporary kitchen. Black countertops and a modular dining island complete the minimalist setting.

OPPOSITE PAGE, BOTTOM Ditching upper cabinets in favor of open shelving is one way to create an unfitted look. These Shaker-style paneled wooden cabinets are a traditional choice that appear modern when paired with glazed subway tiles.

On frameless cabinets, drawer fronts and doors cover the entire front of the case, meeting up with each other at gaps of a fraction of an inch.

Face-Frame or Frameless

In the past, all cabinets were constructed in essentially the same fashion. The storage compartment—called the "case"—had a frame attached to the front to provide rigidity and uniformity across a row of cabinets. Doors were mounted to the frame, either sitting inside of it, so that they were flush with the frame (known as flush-mounted), or attached to the front of the frame (called a partial overlay). The case sat on a riser, which makes room for your feet when you stand up against the counter.

In recent decades, the frameless case—also known as European style—has gained popularity. Doors are attached directly to the front of the case to cover the entire opening. The case is typically made of plywood or MDF masked with strips of laminate or veneer. Because there's no frame for the doors and drawers to sit in or against, this is called a full overlay.

Many door styles are available for both face-frame and frameless cases, though the latter were initially used for more contemporary-styled cabinets. In addition to the simpler construction, which can translate to lower costs, frameless cabinets also have greater interior space. In a framed cabinet, a drawer has to fit inside the frame, wasting space between it and the cabinet walls or the adjacent drawer. But drawers and pullouts in a frameless cabinet use every inch of interior space.

TOP Designed like an antique china cabinet, these face-frame units feature flush-mounted drawers and doors. When glass doors are used, the shelves should align with the cross-pieces, as they do here.

BOTTOM LEFT Drawers and doors that attach to the front of a face-frame cabinet, leaving some of the frame showing between them, are known as a partial overlay.

BOTTOM RIGHT Full-overlay doors and drawers are available in traditional styles, such as these Shaker fronts. While they don't achieve a completely traditional look, full-overlay cases can be economical.

Stock, Semi-Custom, or Custom

Cabinetry falls into three broad categories, according to how it is made and sold:

STOCK CABINETS are mass-produced, sold retail, and come in fixed sizes and a range of finishes. You pick the style and calculate the footage, and the cabinets are quickly dispatched from a warehouse. The least expensive stock cabinets are ready to assemble (RTA). They are sold flat and must be assembled after delivery.

SEMI-CUSTOM CABINETS can be anything from stock cabinets fitted with custom doors to cabinetry that is built to order but chosen from a catalog of available styles and materials.

CUSTOM CABINETS are one of a kind, made for you by a cabinetmaker. As such, they hold no limitations on materials, configurations, accessories, or finishes.

DESIGNER
MARTHA ANGUS ON

Stock vs. Custom

Martha Angus says the choice between stock and custom can "really depend on your budget and how long you'll be in your home. I've seen (stock) kitchens that look incredible!" If longevity isn't a critical issue for you or turnaround time is, and if you've found stock cabinets with the look you want, they could be the sensible choice.

ABOVE Stock cabinets are available in a range of styles and finishes. Here, blond base and pantry cabinets are stylishly paired with stainless-steel uppers and an antique table.

OPPOSITE PAGE, TOP Custom cabinets allow creative solutions, such as this trick door designed to fit the slope of a roof and these arched upper doors that match the window they flank.

OPPOSITE PAGE, BOTTOM For elegant furniture-grade cabinets like these, select paneled doors that mimic the look of your home's existing molding around windows and doors.

These categories aren't necessarily indicators of quality or even price. It's possible to get well-made stock cabinets and poorly made custom ones. A wide array of styles are available in stock and semi-custom outlets, but architect Neal Schwartz cautions that the extra planning, labor, and work-arounds needed to incorporate prefab cabinetry into an existing space can offset any savings. "And besides, custom cabinets don't always cost more than stock cabinets" from a high-quality fabricator, he says. That's because many cabinetmakers farm out construction of the cases to larger operations that can do that part more economically while still meeting your cabinetmaker's specifications.

However, Schwartz believes stock cabinets can be ideal for low-wear or short-term installations. He put custom doors on stock cabinets for his office kitchen, where it isn't imperative that the units last forever. Likewise, when he renovated his home, he spent $300 on stock cabinets for his temporary kitchen, which he used for two and a half years. The cabinets were then moved into his new laundry room, where they are sufficient for the wear they'll get. His long-term kitchen has custom cabinets that were designed to make optimal use of the space and built to last.

Whatever you choose, examine the materials and ask about the construction. Cabinets made of particleboard or those glued or stapled together will not hold up to wear—or to a heavy countertop, as architect Kathryn Rogers notes. "If you put a stone counter on inexpensive stock cabinets, the doors will be hanging off them in a year." Shelves less than ⅝ inch thick will bow over time, as will drawer bottoms made of too-thin particleboard. Doors and drawers should fit squarely on cases, and none of the slides or hinges should stick or squeak.

Materials and Finishes

Like just about everything else, cabinets are now available in a wider variety of materials than ever before. New types of laminate and tempered glass options abound. Rich wood-grain cabinets are hotter than ever and come in a range of hardwoods and veneers. The best news is that you're no longer expected to choose just one style or finish. Today's kitchens mix and match materials and finishes in endless combinations, bringing personality into the kitchen in a whole new way.

One thing to consider when you're shopping for cabinets is the amount of wear and tear they'll endure and the practicality of each material. High-gloss finishes, whether painted or laminate, will reveal fingerprints unless they are wiped down daily. And light colored cabinets will need to be cleaned more frequently than darker options. If you choose wire- or glass-paned cabinets, be ready to keep your kitchen essentials beautifully organized, since they will be on display at all times.

Wood—whether solid wood or a veneer—is still the most popular option for cabinet doors and drawers because it is long lasting and versatile. It's common practice for the box of the cabinet to be crafted from particleboard or plywood, so make sure that face-frame cabinets are finished on the front with a veneer to match the doors.

Think Green

It's not always easy to remain environmentally responsible during home renovations, but luckily there's an ever-growing market for green remodeling solutions. Sustainably harvested materials such as bamboo and FSC-certified woods can be used to either reface or replace your existing cabinets. For the least impact, consider repainting with low- or no-VOC paints to change

the look entirely without introducing new pollutants into your home. If you do buy or commission new cabinets, pay attention to what they're constructed of. There's a host of natural and recycled resin materials that can be used in eco-friendly kitchen cabinets. Traditionally, new cabinet cases are built of plywood, MDF, or other pressed-wood products made with glues containing urea formaldehyde. Formaldehyde off-gases (releases toxins) at a diminishing rate, so older cabinets are safer in that regard than new ones. Some manufacturers now make plywood and MDF products using nontoxic soy-based adhesives, but you will need to specifically request that from your cabinetmaker. There are also water-based, nontoxic wood finishes to stain and seal your cabinets.

Finally, explore your removal options. Having your old cabinets deconstructed, or removed without damage, rather than demolished means you can reuse them in a garage workshop or office, or donate them to a good cause.

TOP Matching cabinets in this kitchen and dining area take on completely different (but still coordinated) looks, thanks to contrasting finishes in black and white and alternating doors in glass and beadboard.

BOTTOM These eco-friendly cabinets by Neil Kelly are constructed with no-added-urea-formaldehyde agriboard, faced with solid alder doors, and finished with low-VOC stain and polyurethane. They are paired with strandwoven bamboo flooring.

Laminates gained
popularity in the mid-
20th century, but they
can still look sleek
(and be cost-effective)
in a modern kitchen.

Smart Storage

If extra eating areas aren't necessary, an island built specifically to add surface area and storage space is a wise investment. This stainless-steel island is chock-full of drawers and cabinets, and it is the centerpiece of this modern kitchen when crowned with a colorful blown-glass chandelier.

As the role of the kitchen grows a little more with each generation, so does the need for specialized storage and work zones. The proliferation of the kitchen island is a great example. What started out as an extra work surface soon became added storage, then an alternative eating area, and today, it's often used as a homework zone. When planning your kitchen cabinetry, be sure to consider your entire household needs.

Islands

A built-in island has become almost mandatory in any new or remodeled kitchen. There's no question that a built-in island, constructed of base cabinets and topped with a wide counter, is a workhorse. It adds to a kitchen's storage capacity and counter space and can be designed to accommodate seating for meals or projects.

If floor space is at a premium and you have to choose between a dining table and an island, give serious thought to how often you eat in your kitchen and whether eating at a counter will work for you. As designer Martha Angus says, "I still don't

like the idea of eating at an island. It just doesn't seem to foster family togetherness, which I think is so important."

The other option a built-in island offers is the ability to locate the sink or stove in the island rather than against the wall. But if you want to use the island as a prep station, as a buffet, or for big projects—even sewing or laundry folding—you may prefer an uninterrupted surface.

If you don't already have an island and you are not planning to bring in a cabinetmaker, consider a freestanding island. Options range from small butcher blocks to stainless-steel restaurant prep tables, antique-style worktables, and large pieces of furniture designed specifically as islands. Look for ones with built-in drawers or a shelf underneath for extra storage. Another option is an island on casters that can be rolled where it's needed or pushed out of the way. Perhaps the biggest benefit of a freestanding island is that it adds a furniture element to an otherwise built-in kitchen, offering a chance for an extra dash of style.

TOP LEFT Extending the countertop along one edge of an island creates seating space without precluding storage. Here, cabinets along the bar side hold less frequently used items like formal dinnerware and large-scale serving pieces.

BOTTOM LEFT Restaurant-supply tables are good island alternatives, especially in narrow spaces. The shelf adds storage.

RIGHT This clever island is something of a hybrid, with an X-base "table" straddling a unit of base cabinets and housing a prep sink. A wine fridge tucks into the other side of the cabinetry .

Work Zones

It is no secret that the kitchen has become command central for most households these days. More often than not, it's where we check our email and charge our phones, keep our calendars and manage the chore schedules. If you're lucky enough to be planning out new cabinets from scratch, don't forget to save room for these kitchen functions.

When you do have the room for a separate eating area in your kitchen, be sure to integrate your cabinet choices. You may not want the upper cabinets to encroach on your dining area, but a length of base cabinets could serve the same purpose as an old-fashioned sideboard. Or consider building a corner hutch to house linens and extra table-top decor.

A small desk area with enough doors and drawers to keep things feeling tidy is a great start. When most of your work happens at the kitchen island, consider dedicating one side to storage for your laptop or craft supplies. An island large enough can serve multiple purposes if planned out correctly. If you don't have the room but need the extra tech support, consider adding a small shelf or cubby within reach of the nearest receptacle to the door. This could be a smart place to keep cell phones charging next to your car keys and wallet.

Room to Grow

If you have an older house with a small room off the kitchen—perhaps it was used as a mudroom or a laundry room or butler's pantry—by all means make that space work triple time for storage by lining it with cabinetry. The style doesn't have to be consistent with the rest of the kitchen. In fact, some designers like to get creative in a pantry or a mudroom, since it's a small, specialized space. A mudroom can feel like an English potting shed with galvanized metal bins

for rain boots, gardening gloves, and dog leashes. A pantry can be turned into a colorful gallery when painted in a bright color, with open shelves and a repetition of the same vessel filled with dry goods. A butler's pantry—typically a short passageway between kitchen and dining room where china and glassware were kept—can be made into a glamorous dressing room for your table with glass-paned cabinets or open shelves.

ABOVE A built-in desk is a common request for kitchen designers. Whether it's incorporated into the rest of the cabinetry or its own special nook, a desk with drawers and cubbies can help keep the eating and cooking surfaces free of clutter.

OPPOSITE PAGE, TOP This spacious kitchen was designed as the home's central living space. Carefully planned to accommo-date all types of tasks, it features specialty storage on the dining side of the island and a small workstation.

OPPOSITE PAGE, BOTTOM An island that's ready for anything—breakfast or crafts for the kids, recipe searches for the cook, and a charging station for phones—requires closed storage and open shelves as well as plenty of receptacles.

Choosing Hardware

Full-extension ball-bearing glides like these allow a drawer to slide smoothly in and out of its slot and be pulled all the way out. Larger drawers for heavier contents require glides rated to handle the weight.

Store-bought or salvaged, trendy or period reproductions, contemporary or traditional, knobs and pulls are available in styles and materials to match any kitchen you might dream up.

Whether it's the knobs and pulls that adorn doors and drawer fronts or the hidden rails that help drawers glide in and out of their slots, hardware elements are the unsung heroes of the kitchen.

If you have the room in your budget to pull out all the stops, consider ingenious extras like telescoping spice racks and pop-up shelves strong enough to hold a countertop mixer. A favorite must-have of the gourmet kitchen is an "appliance garage," which has a roll-down cover to hide items like a coffee maker or toaster that easily slide out on a tray when needed (see pages 160–161).

Knobs, Pulls, and Hinges

Like jewelry for your kitchen, knobs and pulls quickly emphasize the style of the cabinets, and they're relatively easy to change when you want a new look. Options range from round wooden knobs to broad, sleek chrome bars, faceted-glass handles, bronze bin pulls, and a host of other styles and finishes to suit your color scheme and cabinet design. Just make sure that all of your choices are equal to their tasks. A bin pull that will accommodate only a couple of fingertips, for instance, may be inadequate on a large drawer of heavy pots.

For face-frame cabinets, there are a number of hinge styles available, from decorative surface-mounted versions that straddle the fronts of the door and frame to butt hinges that tuck discreetly between them. Frameless cabinets all take concealed hinges that attach to the inside of the cabinet and the backside of the door, so looks aren't a factor. A benefit of the frameless hinge is that minute adjustments can be made to the positioning after it's attached.

Drawer Glides

If you've ever struggled to open and close a drawer while dinner was boiling away on the stove, you know how critical glides can be. The bigger the drawer and the heavier its contents, the more crucial it is that the glides be well made. Options run the gamut from a drawer with no glide, which simply slides into the opening unassisted, to full-extension ball-bearing glides. Newer glides also offer soft-closing mechanisms, which prevent a drawer from slamming shut.

Rethinking the Box

Cabinets provide both the character and the structure of this renovated kitchen, dividing the space into zones while supplying the storage.

Neal Schwartz had big plans for tearing down the original walls of this Victorian-era kitchen and opening up the space to the rear garden. "My original scheme showed a glass conservatory—more open and, admittedly, more modern" than the final plan, he says. But his clients wanted to maintain the three-part layout of the original floor plan, with a main kitchen, a "washroom," and a breakfast nook. In the end, the walls still came down, and up went an artful array of custom cabinets designed to both divide and unify the spaces.

The Elements

- **Cabinets:** Custom white oak

- **Additional Storage:** Walk-in pantry (not shown)

- **Island:** Built of matching cabinetry, with an overhang on one end for seating

- **Hardware:** Classic knobs and wire pulls in brushed nickel

- **Counters:** Honed Pietra Cardosa with mitered edges

- **Backsplash:** Full walls of sage green ceramic, laid in a running bond pattern

- **Sinks:** Custom steel undermount sink with built-in drainboard; two steel undermount bowl sinks in the island

- **Appliances:** All stainless steel; two dishwashers in the washroom

- **Flooring:** Main kitchen is white oak; washroom is narrow strips of French limestone laid in a herring-bone pattern

- **Seating:** Built-in bench with storage

- **Finishing Touches:** Roman shades on two windows; simple white blown-glass light fixtures; streamlined furnishings

Q+A: Architect Neal Schwartz talks about how an uncommon approach to cabinetry led to a kitchen both he and his clients could love.

The layout here harks back to the original kitchen, but you really opened it up. How did you decide to tear down the walls and let cabinetry perform their function?

I originally felt that there was great potential to open up the rear of the house dramatically to the garden, but there was much discussion about how to maintain the traditional feel of the house and its spaces. The idea of the separate "washroom" was not a concept I brought to the project. I feared it would break up the kitchen severely and might lead to a redundancy of functions— double trash bins, double sinks, double coffeemakers. But the idea took hold with the clients, so it became my job to meet their goals while avoiding an overly divided floor plan.

I didn't want the decision to diminish the potential quality of the space, hence the idea to do away with the newly imagined washroom's walls and replace them with cabinetry. We conceived of it as a box of cabinetry that happened to be sitting in the larger room. Then we aligned a series of "windows" through the cabinetry.

The cabinets have a distinctive look.

They were designed to reference both traditional and modern aesthetics. The detailing is subtle and meant to be read in both ways. For example, there is a reference to the traditional frame-and-panel construction of the doors, but it's achieved with a small reveal in a more modern-feeling (full-overlay) door. The trick was to draw from both eras to create something unique to the house.

How much does your cabinetry design follow your clients' belongings and behaviors, and how much is just smart design?

These clients were coming from a house that had a too-small kitchen and ill-conceived storage, so thinking through every element was crucial. We labeled every drawer and had the clients measure practically every pot and pan. The request for the plate racks came from the clients and was specific to their way of living. The pullout "pantry" cabinet was a challenge because it is at the threshold between the kitchen and the washroom. No storage solution seemed to make sense for both spaces. I finally thought of the idea of splitting it down the middle. One side became perfect for cooking spices and small supplies, leaving the other side for coffee and teas. In a kitchen, there isn't a lot of architectural ego in terms of storage—it simply has to work.

How did you choose the tile and treatment for that stove wall and window frames?

I felt like there was a lot going on in the kitchen and it was a wall that could use something bold but simple, so we just chose a really beautiful tile that would look good with the warmth of the oak. And I felt strongly about trying to create one room that happened to be divided by cabinetry, so we wrapped it into the washroom as well, for that continuity. With the stove and the grease and everything along there, doing the window frames in tile seemed like the cleanest, simplest way to deal with that whole wall. Plus, wrapping the tile around the window frames makes it seem more like a thick stone wall and less like thin tile glued to a wall.

The floor in the washroom is exquisite. Why did you do a different floor in there?

Honestly? I went into a showroom and they had that exact stone laid in that herringbone pattern and I thought it was incredibly beautiful, and I just wanted to use it. It would have been overpowering in the larger space, but it seemed like in the tiny washroom we could get away with a little bit of extravagance. It amuses me that this space we were calling the washroom— as if it were the back room of a farmhouse—has the nicest floor, the nicest cabinetry, the nicest view.

You've inset smaller slabs of the counter stone in the pass-through and the shelf across from the island. What prompted that?

I was just tying the spaces together with some of the detailing. Anything big enough to be a countertop felt like an appropriate use of that material.

Why two sinks in the island?

The husband in this family does most of the cooking, so he has his sink across from the stove. On the opposite side of the island from the washroom is a walk-in pantry along with the refrigerator, a small desk, the microwave, and so on. The wife tends to use that space, dealing with the kids and all, so she has a sink as well. In this case, the island is big enough for a couple of workstations, and it made sense that each would have its own sink.

What's your philosophy on finishing touches?

In general, life heads toward entropy. I try to be conscious that I'm just a background influence and that a lot is going to happen in the space once I'm done. So I prefer to pick a few simple, beautiful materials and let life fill in the rest.

BEFORE

The partition between the cooking station and the washroom is actually a pullout pantry, with appropriate supplies on each side.

MIDDLE RIGHT The breakfast nook borrows an extra window from the washroom, thanks to a perfectly aligned pass-through.

BOTTOM RIGHT Double dishwashers and ample dish storage, including built-in plate racks, make the washroom efficient. The herringbone floor lends big character to the little space.

Historical Hybrid

THIS PAGE Price says the kitchen's solid-front top drawers are "a pretty traditional detail. They used a single piece of wood whenever possible, but beyond about 6 or 8 inches it got too pricey." Less traditional are the frameless base cabinets, but face-frame construction was used for focal points such as the full-height glass-front cabinet and the asymmetrical open uppers.

OPPOSITE PAGE, TOP Tucked behind the cabinets that divide the dining room and kitchen is a small bar, easily accessed from either side.

OPPOSITE PAGE, BOTTOM The new layout, flowing toward a glass door and casement windows at the breakfast end of the room, established a relationship with the backyard that was nonexistent before.

The galley kitchen of this 1918 Craftsman bungalow was widened by just 18 inches and elongated by 8 feet, making room for a desk, a breakfast table, and doorways to the family room and backyard at the far end. The new cabinets are all custom built, but architect Kevin Price achieved cost savings by combining face-frame and frameless cases. "The face-frame cabinets have the more historical look, but they cost more because they're more labor intensive. So we used them where your eye tends to land—on the uppers—and then went with frameless cabinets everywhere else."

The Elements

- **Cabinets:** Painted hybrid of face-frame and frameless cases with flush-mounted and full-overlay fronts, respectively; Shaker-style doors and drawers except for plain-front top drawers

- **Additional Built-ins:** Desk and hutch built of cabinet components; breakfast bench built to match cabinets

- **Hardware:** Oil-rubbed bronze wire pulls and turn-locks

- **Counters:** Honed black granite with eased edge; cherry desktop and tabletop

- **Backsplash:** White oversized handmade subway tiles in running bond pattern with decorative inlay above stove

- **Sink:** White apron sink with gooseneck faucet

- **Appliances:** Stainless-steel stove, hood, and built-in convection microwave; refrigerator and dishwasher with front panels to match cabinetry

- **Flooring:** Linoleum

- **Finishing Touches:** Soft green, khaki, and yellow palette; bracket detailing on upper cabinets and open shelves; casement windows; vintage-style light fixtures; chalkboard paint on wall above desk; classic Navy chairs

Chapter 3

Counters and Backsplashes

No matter how beautiful your kitchen is, it's ultimately a utility space
—meant to be worked in. Although it's easy to get swept up in the
abundance of counter and backsplash options available these days,
and while your choice of work surfaces and wall treatments will go
a long way toward establishing the look you're after, don't lose sight
of the fact that counters and backsplashes have a job to do.

Choosing kitchen
materials can be a
fun mix-and-match
project. A thin marble
slab counter is paired
with white tiles on
the backsplash for
surprisingly affordable

Counter Considerations

There is more to choosing a countertop than simply complementing the style of your cabinets—it must also meet your functional needs. That means supporting the tasks of cooking—standing up to knives, hot pots, rolling pins, and spills—as well as lending itself to cleanup and maintenance routines that you can live with.

Counter Types

A counter can come in many forms. It might be a slab cut from natural stone or manufactured in materials ranging from engineered stone to high-tech plastics to composites containing recycled glass or paper. It might be wood, in either butcher-

block or plank form. It might be plywood that's been surfaced with a laminate, wrapped in stainless steel, or tiled. Or it might be concrete poured in place. And those are just some of the most popular options.

Slab-style counters, particularly stone slabs, are a time-tested favorite for both contemporary kitchens and historical renovations. Stone has proved popular, thanks to its practical traits: strength, durability, heat and moisture resistance, and a wipe-clean surface. The continuous seamless surface of a slab counter makes daily cleanup a cinch, although stone surfaces still require periodic maintenance.

OPPOSITE PAGE This kitchen has stained butcher block on the island, hard-wearing stainless steel beside the stove, and elegant granite everywhere else. The similar color of the steel and granite and the warm contrast of wood at the room's center prevent a crazy-quilt look.

TOP RIGHT Poured concrete is an earthy, modern option for counters. Because it has to be resealed periodically, concrete is durable but far from indestructible, so cutting boards and quick cleanup of spills are required.

BOTTOM RIGHT It's OK to mix materials, even on a single surface. One end of this island is capped in a marble slab for working with dough. The perimeter counter is stainless steel with a raised front rim and an integrated sink.

Wood, concrete, and steel also have minimal seams and are gaining in popularity, but don't rule out tile without considering its advantages. Tile comes in a vast array of colors, shapes, sizes, and materials—including marble mosaics and stainless-steel "bricks." Tile's vulnerability is its grout, which can stain, erode, or chip over time, but technology in grout and its sealants has improved in recent years. If you're going for a retro look, tile may achieve a more authentic effect, and most tile can be laid by moderately handy homeowners.

The Right Surface for the Job

Do you like to chop directly on your countertop or set hot pots on it? Are you willing to wax or seal the surface routinely? Will nicks and stains bother or charm you? How about water spots and fingerprints? The right surface for you depends on how you prioritize these matters.

Marble, for example, has long been favored by bakers because its cool surface is ideal for working with dough. However, it's susceptible to staining and is eroded by the acids in food and wine. Many people choose marble for its looks and because they want a surface that will age and weather, but if stains and surface inconsistencies will bother you, consider a more rugged material.

The good news is that you needn't limit yourself to one kind of surface. You might choose polished granite for perimeter counters and butcher block for the island, or concrete counters with a marble inset as a pastry-making station, or even handsome wood counters with more durable soapstone around the sink. The possibilities are endless, so pick materials that match your varying criteria, then situate them accordingly. The mix-and-match strategy can also offer budgetary help if you choose materials of varying price points. For instance, the owners of the kitchen on pages 14–15 used retro-chic plastic laminate with metal edging for their long counter and pricier quartz on their island.

Counter Materials

Because water is the enemy of wood, this mahogany counter has an inset around the sink—marble with an integrated drainboard.

In weighing your countertop options, look beyond style and price to issues of installation, durability, and maintenance (both short and long term). And since most counter materials will outlast your kitchen's next remodel, it's wise to also consider aspects of removal and reusability.

Laminate

The most widely available and least expensive counter option, laminate consists of a thin sheet of polymer glued onto a substrate of plywood or particleboard. Often the front and side edges are faced with separate strips of laminate, creating vulnerable corner seams, but the counter can also be edged in wood or metal for better durability. Laminate comes in a wide variety of solid colors and patterns, as well as photo reproductions of wood or stone. It is somewhat stain resistant, and the better varieties have through-body color, so scratches are less apparent. But laminate is easily scratched and not heat resistant, and damage can't be repaired.

This surface is quicker and easier to install than others. You can find counters designed specifically for do-it-yourselfers that are molded with an integrated backsplash and seamless rounded fore-edge and sold by the linear foot.

Tile

Tile is available in a vast range of styles and materials—including ceramic, glass, stone, steel, concrete, and handmade specialty tiles—some of which have recycled content. But not all tile is suitable for countertops, where you'll want something hard, dense, and smooth. Tile counters can be edged in wood or metal but are most often edged in matching trim tile. Grout lines make for an irregular surface, so no matter which material you choose, you'll want to have a cutting board handy and perhaps a slab of marble for rolling dough. Glazed ceramic tile is the most common option. It's durable, unfazed by heat or water, and easily wipes clean. But the grout between tiles is less durable and can require periodic sealing.

Even in equivalent material, tile is cheaper than essentially any slab counter. All countertop materials are priced by the square foot, and while a square foot of granite tile, for example, costs more than basic ceramic tile, it costs substantially less than a square foot of slab granite. So if you love the look of granite but are on a tight budget, opt for granite tiles.

Tile is also a good option for do-it-yourselfers, depending on the tile and the complexity of the installation, and repairs can be simpler. If a slab cracks, it has to be replaced entirely, whereas a cracked tile can be chiseled out and replaced. With any tile job, buy extra and store it to ensure a perfect match.

ABOVE Laminate comes in many colors and patterns, including this wood-grain variety. Metal edging adds to the retro look.

RIGHT Traditional glazed ceramic tile counters are usually edged in matching trim tiles. Here, white ceramic squares were set on the diagonal.

BELOW A tiled surface extends the usefulness of the wooden kitchen island in this vintage-style country kitchen. It's more water-resistant than a wooden counter, and it serves as an easy-to-clean breakfast bar.

TOP LEFT Paired with wraparound open shelving and a stainless drainboard sink, well-sealed wooden counters maintain visual consistency in this compact country kitchen.

TOP RIGHT Concrete can be made to suit even a cottage-style kitchen. To save on installation costs, and with the help of a knowledgeable friend, this homeowner poured her own counters.

BOTTOM Among the many benefits of stainless steel is that it allows for the sink and counter to be one truly seamless surface.

Wood and Bamboo

Wooden counters range from planks of reclaimed pine to pristine teak or butcher block. Traditional "end grain" butcher block is actually made up of small lengths of maple glued together so that the cut ends create the hardest possible surface. Most retail butcher-block countertops are "edge grain," which is not as hard but less porous than end grain. Face-grain (plank) options are not suitable as cutting surfaces. Eco-friendly bamboo is technically a grass and is therefore much softer than a true wood. Opt for strand-woven bamboo, which is manufactured for extra strength, if you want to cut on your counter. All wood cutting surfaces should be treated periodically with food-safe oil; non-food surfaces should be sealed with a water-based, low-VOC sealant. Moisture and humidity warp and discolor wood, so it's best used away from sinks and dishwashers. Scratches, food stains, and rings left by hot pots can all be sanded out.

Concrete

Extremely versatile, concrete can be colored, textured, inlaid, and molded—meaning it can be made to suit any style of kitchen. Counters are either cast off-site and installed by the fabricator or are poured in place. Concrete is heavy and temperamental, so only intrepid homeowners should attempt installing it themselves. It is also best for those who like a patina, since it's subject to stains and prone to hairline cracks. A penetrating sealer will preserve concrete's heat-proof nature but won't make it stain resistant. Topical sealant and periodic waxing will make it stain resistant. Make sure your floor and cabinets can take the weight, and bear in mind that removing concrete counters is no small job. Somewhat lighter and less expensive, fiber-cement counters are made from a mix of concrete and cellulose fiber.

Stainless Steel

Stainless-steel work surfaces are gaining in popularity for all the reasons restaurants rely on them: They are resistant to heat, water, rust, and bacteria and are easy to clean. They also allow for the sink and backsplash to be truly integral, eliminating vulnerable seams. Look for heavy-duty steel (14–16 gauge) wrapped around plywood or MDF, both for durability and to reduce noise. Be aware that only chrome-nickel blends are truly "stainless." Other metals—such as copper, zinc, and aluminum—are also available but can be higher maintenance. Metal counters are generally self-edged. You'll have the choice of a squared or rounded edge, or a tiny raised front rim to contain water.

Insets and Cutouts

When is a countertop more than a countertop? When it's also a drainboard, knife block, trivet, cutting board, or hatch door.

ABOVE Stone, synthetic, and concrete counters that sit higher than the sink can have integrated drainboards.

RIGHT A niche can be carved out of nearly any surface to accommodate a contrasting one. Here, marble is inset with a wooden cutting board that lifts out for transport and cleanup.

BELOW LEFT Discreet slits allow knives to be stored right at the cutting surface. Metal strips can also be applied to any solid countertop for a built-in trivet.

BELOW RIGHT A cutout for a rim and lid provides easy access to a trash can stored in the cabinet below.

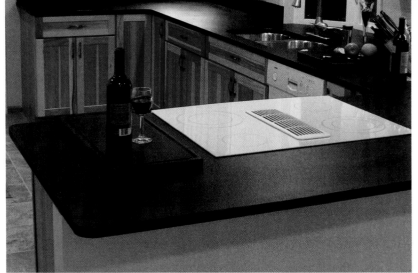

Synthetic Slabs

"Solid surface" products are crafted of a mineral compound suspended in polyester or acrylic resin (aka plastic). "Engineered stone" results from a process that replicates the formation of naturally occurring stone, using quartz or granite and resin. Both come in a broad range of colors and patterns. More important, they've been engineered to provide the optimum work surface—durable, nonporous, low maintenance, and highly resistant to bacteria, water, and heat—but with varying degrees of success. Some solid surface materials can be scorched by a hot pot, but a light buffing with a rough sponge will fix small surface imperfections. Like stainless steel, synthetics allow for a truly integrated sink or backsplash, eliminating seams altogether.

Synthetic slabs are available with edge profiling similar to that of stone slabs, but fancier cuts cost more. None of them look exactly like stone, but they can be worth the trade-off from a maintenance or cost perspective. Not all synthetics are less expensive than stone.

Recycled and "Green" Composites

Composite countertops made of eco-friendly materials are increasingly available on the market. However, the environmental benefits of these products vary—as do their durability and longevity—so pay attention to the specifics. One product might use recycled matter (glass and paper are common) but bind it with a non-biodegradable, petroleum-based resin. Another might use material that's not recycled but is certified sustainable, and suspend it in a natural resin. Some composite materials use a combination of concrete and fly ash, which minimizes the amount of cement needed and diverts the fly ash from the landfill. In researching your options, ask questions about the entire life span of the product: whether the content is recycled and what it's suspended in, whether the manufacturing process is nontoxic and local, whether the end product emits any noxious gasses, and whether the counters are recyclable or biodegradable. If the sales material boasts that the structure of the product "cannot be altered," it's not likely to biodegrade.

Recycled metals are also on the rise. The manufacture of metal is hard on the environment and metal is not a renewable resource, but the upside is that it's a hygienic surface and is endlessly recyclable without any downgrading. It's important to remember that the most eco-friendly counters are still those that are made from natural, renewable materials and whose end product is both recyclable and biodegradable—which is why wood, when responsibly harvested and treated, is still widely considered the most earth-friendly choice.

TOP PaperStone is made of FSC-certified recycled paper in non-petroleum, non-formaldehyde resin. It boasts integral color and is heat and stain resistant.

MIDDLE IceStone, which suspends 100 percent recycled glass in portland cement, offers sustainable surfaces manufactured in the United States. It consists of colored glass shards mixed with natural pigments.

BOTTOM Using post-industrial aluminum shavings embedded in either acrylic or polyester, Alkemi incorporates recycled metal into a glittery solid surface material perfect for countertops.

A modern kitchen looks as sleek as a race car, with shiny cabinets and white countertops. The solid surface material has an integrated sink basin, and it wraps up the wall to create a seamless backsplash.

In this chic urban kitchen, thick white marble tops a black island while honed black granite—which calls to mind classic laboratory counters—tops the white base cabinets.

Natural Stone

The colors and types of stone that are available for countertops are too numerous to list, but the most popular options are granite, marble, soapstone, and slate. These vary in their softness, porosity, and stain resistance, so require different levels of care, but all are extremely durable. Thanks to its varied selection, stone can be equally at home in a loft or a farmhouse. When choosing counters, you'll have to decide about the edge shape (or profile)—see the illustration below—as well as the finish. A honed surface is smoothed and sealed but not polished, while a polished surface has a glassy finish. Stone is generally the most expensive counter option, but cost varies by the type and thickness of the stone and where it is quarried (both for the quality of the quarry's stone and how far it must travel). Stone, of course, is heavy, so be sure to determine whether your floor and cabinets can support it.

Matters of wear and patina are more important with stone than perhaps with any other surface. How you treat, maintain, and feel about your counters will determine what kind of stone you go with and whether you'll battle or welcome the signs of age and wear. Architect Kathryn Rogers starts by making sure that her clients will be happy with stone. "You don't want to spend a bunch of money and then be disappointed in five years" if it doesn't look like new anymore, she says. The aesthetic value between the granularity of a rosy granite versus the veining of a Carrara marble is in the eye of the beholder. Kevin Price, for example, says, "I love granite for its monolithic qualities and its wear-resistance, and it's more economical than soapstone. But soapstone weathers over time and has a richness and patina that are really wonderful." Rogers adds that soapstone hides stains and that its warmth makes it better suited to old houses than granite, but he allows that some people find it too dark. Neal Schwartz's favorite stone is an Italian schist called Pietra Cardosa, because the rich veining immediately conveys that it's a natural material and that every piece is unique.

Unless you're visiting the quarry and picking the exact piece of stone your counter will be cut from, expect that the stone you get will vary slightly from the sample you're shown by your architect or retailer. The color, granularity, or veining will differ from quarry to quarry and piece to piece—that's just the nature of stone.

With its characteristic honed finish and subtle veining, soapstone has a much softer nature than marble or granite, and it ages beautifully.

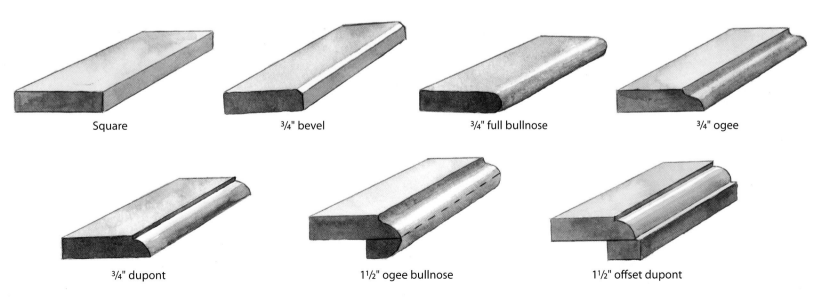

Square   ¾" bevel   ¾" full bullnose   ¾" ogee

¾" dupont   1½" ogee bullnose   1½" offset dupont

CLOCKWISE FROM LEFT
Concrete brings a different kind of earthiness than stone and can also be stained, molded, and inlaid.

Butcher block is a true workhorse of a surface and also naturally anti-microbial.

Solid-surface materials are more economical than stone and can hold up better to wear.

Counters at a glance

Laminate

- **Assets:** Wide array of colors and patterns. Inexpensive, readily available, easy to install (including DIY). Wipes clean.

- **Price:** $

- **Maintenance:** Edge seams susceptible to water damage. Somewhat stain resistant but easily scratched. Damage cannot be repaired. If substrate contains urea formaldehyde, seal any exposed areas to minimize off-gassing. (Ask about non-formaldehyde options.)

- **Green Issues:** Laminate counters have a relatively short life span but can be easily removed and repurposed, or tiled over.

Tile

- **Assets:** Durable and waterproof when glazed or sealed. An option for do-it-yourselfers, depending on the specifics of the installation.

- **Price:** $–$$

- **Maintenance:** Stone and concrete tile require sealing. Grout is subject to staining and also requires sealing. Ask if more durable epoxy grout is an option for you.

- **Green Issues:** Tile can be laid directly over some existing counters, saving them from the landfill.

Wood

- **Assets:** Naturally antibacterial. Stains and scratches can be sanded out. Won't dull knives. Suitable for do-it-yourselfers.

- **Price:** $–$$$

- **Maintenance:** Treat cutting surfaces with food-safe oil (mineral, linseed, or tung). If a non-food surface will be sealed in your home rather than at the factory, ask for water-based, low-VOC sealant. Keep wood surfaces as dry as possible.

- **Green Issues:** Wood is a renewable resource—look for sustainably harvested products—and can be recycled.

Concrete

- **Assets:** Highly versatile in color, style, and finish. Naturally heat resistant.

- **Price:** $$–$$$

- **Maintenance:** Topical sealants can increase stain resistance but are damaged by heat and knives. Concrete should be waxed periodically.

- **Green Issues:** While a concrete counter won't be easy to remove, it can be recycled.

Stainless Steel

- **Assets:** Hard-wearing; resistant to water, rust, heat, and bacteria.
- **Price:** $$–$$$
- **Maintenance:** Can be dented and scratched —never cut directly on it—and shows fingerprints and water spots if not thoroughly dried. That's less true of brushed or matte finishes than polished or mirrored ones.
- **Green Issues:** Metal is energy-intensive to produce and is not renewable, but it can be recycled and often contains recycled material.

Synthetic Slabs

- **Assets:** Durable and low maintenance; nonporous, resistant to water, heat, and bacteria.
- **Price:** $$$–$$$$
- **Maintenance:** Damaged spots can be easily buffed out of most products.
- **Green Issues:** Look for a composite slab made of recycled material bound in a non-toxic resin or concrete and finish it with low-VOC sealants or wax.

Stone

- **Assets:** Beautiful, natural, and durable. Can be treated to maintain pristine qualities or encouraged to patina over time.
- **Price:** $$$$
- **Maintenance:** Honed surfaces require regular sealing. Most kinds of damage can be sanded out.
- **Green Issues:** To limit the carbon footprint, choose a stone that's quarried close to home.

Engineered stone can be more durable than natural stone and is antibacterial, but it can cost just as much as the real thing.

Backsplashes

Blue glass tiles arranged in a familiar subway pattern extend from counter to ceiling, offering a cool backdrop for stainless-steel appliances, marble counters and classic white trim.

It's uncommon to see a kitchen in which the countertop meets the wall with nothing but a little caulk at the junction. That's because a kitchen wall is subject to standing water on the countertops, splashing water from the sink, and splattering food from all directions. So it's traditional to treat it with a protective—and often decorative—covering.

Partial Backsplashes

The most basic backsplash is a simple curb a few inches tall—either integral to the countertop or a separate strip of matching or contrasting material. It could be a band of well-sealed wood, a strip of stainless steel, or a row of decorative tile. If you decide on a short backsplash, paint the wall above it with latex paint in a semigloss or gloss finish that will hold up to scrubbing, since you're likely to wash the wall from time to time.

More common is a backsplash that runs up to the bottom of the windows or upper cabinets, creating a uniform surface in that in-between space. Essentially any material that is water and heat resistant—and reasonably easy to wipe clean—is suitable, which means the

range of options is much wider than for work surfaces. And because the square footage of a backsplash tends to be small, even high-end materials can be affordable. Given all of that, the backsplash is an ideal spot to get creative, and to bring color and texture into your kitchen.

Tile has long been the backsplash material of choice—the range of styles, patterns, and materials available seems endless—but today's kitchens also incorporate sheet materials such as glass, laminate and stainless steel. Newer tile options include natural stone cut to various sizes as well as shimmering mosaic glass and steel tiles, many of which have recycled content. When choosing your backsplash, remember to think long term: Ask yourself if the tile you love today will still appeal to you five or 10 years down the line. And if you're renovating with the intent to sell, stick to neutrals. As designer Martha Angus says, "It doesn't make sense to do a bold color or bold design, because it may not appeal to a future buyer."

TOP A boldly hued laminate can be used as an accent in an all-white kitchen, and it can be easily swapped out when it's time to refinish the cabinets.

BOTTOM Tile comes in countless materials and ready-made patterns. This marble herringbone was used to complement a kitchen with slab marble counters.

ARCHITECT KATHRYN ROGERS ON

Tiled Backsplashes

If you're putting a new kitchen in an old house, ceramic tile counters might be appropriate. But if you prefer slab counters, Kathryn Rogers says, "Do a tile backsplash—that way you get the best of both worlds."

Full-Wall Backsplashes

Functionally speaking, only the lower part of your wall needs to be water-proof. However, there are few ways to make a more dramatic statement than to tile a full wall, even if it's in simple white subway tile. This is an increasingly popular approach, especially in kitchens that have no upper cabinets to establish a clear stopping point for a partial backsplash. But even if you have uppers, think about tiling the space above them as well as below. Just keep in mind that what might make for a nice pop of color on a partial back-splash could be overwhelming on a full wall, so consider just how dramatic you want to be.

Remember, too, that full-wall treatments needn't be limited to tile. Slabs of natural stone as well as sheets of glass or steel can cover as large a stretch of wall as your desires and budget warrant.

TOP ROW In a kitchen inspired by an old-fashioned checkered taxi, the backsplash becomes the focal point.

An enormous slab of dramatically veined white marble makes a stunning wall treatment behind this classic French range.

Blond cabinets, soft gray walls, and deep gray concrete counters get a jolt of color from this backsplash of hand-tooled tiles in vivid yellow.

BOTTOM ROW A full wall of creamy subway tiles adds to the subtle drama of this old-world space.

Green glass mosaic tile was applied here, not just to the wall below and above the cabinets but to the front of the peninsula as well.

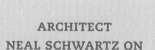

ARCHITECT
NEAL SCHWARTZ ON

Tiled Walls

With his aesthetic of "a few materials used really well," Neal Schwartz finds backsplashes "vexing." Given the variety of elements and contents innate to a kitchen, a partial backsplash can seem like one treatment too many. His preferred approach is to tile the whole wall instead of breaking it into wall and backsplash, thereby keeping the number and types of surfaces to a minimum.

Concrete Notions

A rear counter of polished stainless steel, with integrated sink and backsplash, is a single dazzling counterpoint to the concrete and wood elements at the heart of this kitchen.

Enlisted to create a "poetic" little beach retreat for an interior designer, Bobby McAlpine devised a space of Zen-like tranquility by relying on neutral tones and humble materials. At the heart of it all are a dining table and a kitchen island—a matched pair rendered in concrete—that speak to both symmetry and ruggedness and take the inherent messiness of kitchen life in stride. "To me," McAlpine says, "kitchens need to be almost church-like to counter the (messy) reality."

The Elements

- **Island:** Taupe-tinted concrete "table" over base cabinets

- **Perimeter Counter:** Polished stainless steel

- **Backsplash:** Integral to steel counter

- **Sinks:** Large integral single-basin main sink; custom wooden prep sink on island

- **Cabinets:** Custom frameless, painted cabinets with grooved fronts

- **Additional Storage:** Floating shelves; wall of pantry closets (not shown)

- **Hardware:** Brushed nickel pulls

- **Appliances:** Gas cooktop; stainless-steel wall oven, dishwasher, trash compactor, and refrigerator (not shown)

- **Flooring:** Concrete

- **Seating:** Concrete table identical to island, with slipcovered side chairs

- **Finishing Touches:** Neutral palette; recessed lighting; bamboo blind

Q+A: Bobby McAlpine talks about his idea of the perfect kitchen, as well as what makes him want to "scream and run."

This concrete-wrapped island and matching table are a statement-making pair. How did you come up with them?
The table and the island are identical, so they're symmetrical as you come in the main entry, one on either side. The symmetry was the concept there.

They also tie into the concrete floor, but then you used polished steel for the back counter rather than more concrete.
The tables really needed to be the more precious device. I wanted to make the space as non-kitchen-y as it could be, so one is the table you cook on and the other is the table you eat on. It would have harmed that idea to continue using concrete on the back counter.

After the counters, the real conversation piece is the wooden sink on the island. Can you tell us about that?
This house has a very Zen feeling to it, and giving the kitchen a low center, with the island and table, leans toward that elegance. But it puts the island at dining height, which is below working height. So setting the sink on top brings it up to working height.

What's the trick to making such slender shelves, like the ones above the backsplash, support weight?
Anytime you're doing that, the shelves have to be cantilevered out of the wall, so they're on steel pins and have to be planned ahead, while the house and the wall are being assembled. I really loathe cabinetry and avoid it every chance I get, because it's the first thing that comes back to haunt you, by dating the space. So I tend to sidestep cabinetry and use shelves and pantries and other devices that are more timeless and won't tell on me later on.

This layout—one wall and an island—is so sensible for people who want an open kitchen. It seems to be a layout you use fairly often in your work.
I think the perfect kitchen has a walk-in pantry at one end of the aisle—or both ends. But this house is tiny, so the pantry became a thinner device—a series of closets instead of a walk-in. In this house a walk-in would be kind of ridiculous: it would be the size of a bathroom. I do prefer a walk-in, though, because the minute you walk in, you see all your stuff—it's not behind closed doors.

Did the owner of this beach house—Betsy Brown, an interior designer—give you free rein with the kitchen's design?
Certainly. The commission in this case was for as poetic an environment as we could create, given the limitations of the site, and Betsy didn't want to do anything or say anything that would compromise it in any way. She wanted the vision, wanted something really lovely and special, and she wanted the pleasure of being given that.

You settled on an all-neutral palette.
She likes neutrals and has a masculine attitude toward color and its use. She tends to use it monolithically. She likes those environments: very quiet.

Of course, the neutrality here contributes to that overall Zen feel of the space, along with the symmetry and the rustic materials.
Kitchens are naturally chaotic because of the activity and the products and all the stuff. And because of that I tend to enlist symmetry to a fault, and I concentrate on trying to calm the nerves of it and to create tremendous visual and emotional order. The great fault of a lot of kitchens is that they are very talkative and express everything they're doing. They're just so proud of everything they've got—you know, when the hood's over there doing jumping jacks and all. It makes me want to scream and run. I think it's better when a kitchen holds its tongue a little bit, tucks some things under its skirt.

What's with the one tiny window in the kitchen?
The one window is just the poetic solitary device—the singular as opposed to the collective. The enormous wall (of windows) is the collective, the release out into the world. The little one is like a little painting.

TOP The spare concrete dining table is an exact match to the shell of the island. McAlpine prefers color to be integral to the materials rather than applied, which makes tinted concrete appealing to him.

BOTTOM LEFT The custom prep sink is clever on a number of levels. Several inches tall and sitting atop the table-height island, it provides a cutting surface at counter height.

BOTTOM RIGHT The kitchen's low ceiling creates a sense of enclosure, but across the dining table is a full wall of glass.

A Grand Plan

THIS PAGE Everything in this kitchen is sized in keeping with its scale, including the end-grain butcher-block countertop on the island, which is 3 inches thick.

OPPOSITE PAGE, LEFT The service kitchen can be closed off behind pocket doors when necessary.

OPPOSITE PAGE, RIGHT This built-in hutch contains plenty of open and closed storage for dinnerware, serving pieces, and table linens.

Though this kitchen—with an adjacent service kitchen and full butler's pantry—is undeniably grand, it's also quite friendly. That's due largely to the soft limestone surfaces, the rustic wood elements, and the charming backsplash. In the main kitchen, behind the 60-inch range, the backsplash runs all the way to the cathedral ceiling. Rendered in 10-inch tiles, which are normally reserved for floors, the backsplash is an oversized mosaic of green, gray, tan, and taupe that sets the tone for the whole space.

The Elements

- **Counters:** Limestone perimeter counters; butcher-block inset with limestone on island

- **Backsplash:** Limestone band with ledge; wall of 10-inch ceramic squares in running bond pattern; matching rectangles in pantry and service kitchen

- **Sinks:** Copper farmhouse sink in main kitchen; ceramic undermount sinks in pantry and service kitchen; exposed bridge faucets

- **Cabinets:** Green-stained face-frame cases with flush-mounted drawers and frame-and-panel doors

- **Hardware:** Blackened bronze bin pulls, knobs, and wire pulls

- **Island:** Cabinet-based with footrail and basket-lined open shelving along front

- **Additional Storage:** Built-in hutches; pot rack above island; adjacent butler's pantry and service kitchen

- **Appliances:** Paneled refrigerator and dishwashers; professional-grade stainless-steel range; copper hood

- **Flooring:** Tumbled limestone with wood inlay

- **Seating:** Barstools at island; oversized table and matching benches

- **Finishing Touches:** Gray-green and brown color palette; exposed beams and rustic paneling; industrial light fixtures on pot rack; casement windows

THIS PAGE A copper sink complements the pots on the combination pot rack and light fixture. The sink is bordered by limestone, which is set into the butcher block.

OPPOSITE PAGE, TOP Between the expanse of wall tile and the limestone counter is a matching limestone band topped with a ledge just deep enough for oils and spices (see page 76).

OPPOSITE PAGE, BOTTOM The front of the island hosts storage baskets and a footrail.

Earthy and Elegant

THIS PAGE Durable terra-cotta tile is the natural choice for both the floor and countertop in this elegantly earthy kitchen.

OPPOSITE PAGE, LEFT The standard corner cabinet problem was solved here with a door placed on the outside. This also allows the dishwasher to tuck in next to it on the opposite side of the peninsula.

OPPOSITE PAGE, RIGHT The wall dividing the kitchen from the front hall is actually a pantry closet, packing lots of storage into the small space.

This tiny home shows its Japanese and California Craftsman influences most prominently in the doors and windows in the combined dining-kitchen space. The perfect match for them, sharing their handcrafted character, is the terra-cotta tile used for the kitchen counters and floor. A tansu in the dining area emphasizes the Japanese influence while providing needed storage.

The Elements

- **Counters:** Self-edged terra-cotta tile

- **Backsplash:** Single row of matching tile with wood edging

- **Cabinets:** Oak veneer with glass doors in upper cabinets

- **Additional Storage:** Wall closet pantry; freestanding Japanese tansu in dining area

- **Hardware:** Blackened steel wire pulls

- **Sink:** Double-basin white ceramic

- **Appliances:** Basic white refrigerator, range, and dishwasher (not shown)

- **Flooring:** Terra-cotta tile

- **Seating:** Understated table with chairs of dark brown webbing

- **Finishing Touches:** Traditional rug; exposed beams; recessed lights in lowered kitchen ceiling; handcrafted French doors and windows

THIS PAGE AND OPPO-SITE PAGE, BOTTOM
The tansu in the dining room complements the architec-tural character of the home. Its myriad compartments hold serving pieces, glassware, table linens, candlesticks, and a host of other necessities.

OPPOSITE PAGE, TOP
Plenty of glass keeps this efficient little kitchen from feeling as small as it is.

Chapter 4

Sinks and Faucets

You may think that choosing a kitchen sink is an easy decision—and faucets may never cross your mind—but it's extremely important to get this duo right. The type of sink you choose will dictate the type of faucet, how the counter is formed, and how all three are installed, so changing your mind later can be a big deal. Plus, most people use their sinks every day, so you want to pick one (or more) that suits all your needs.

A double-basin apron sink fitted with twin faucets is a clever plan for harmonious side-by-side kitchen duty. One person can be rinsing vegetables while another loads the dishwasher.

Sinks

A good sink is a surprisingly personal choice. On top of style and material, you need to think about the size and number of basins and whether you will want a drainboard for your primary washing-up zone. Also consider whether you have the room for and interest in an additional prep sink.

Types and Materials

Sinks are described by the way they are installed in relation to the counter. Material choices vary by sink type: **DROP-IN (OR OVERMOUNT)** sinks fit in a hole in the counter and have an overlapping rim that can be sealed. The faucet,

sprayer, and any other accessories are typically mounted to predrilled holes in the sink, so the type of faucet you choose will need to match up with the number and spacing of the holes. Drop-in sinks are generally enameled cast iron or stainless steel and are the easiest type to install. **UNDERMOUNT** sinks attach to the underside of a cutout in a slab-style counter, so the counter forms the rim, which makes it easy to sweep crumbs and water into the sink. The faucet and other accessories are attached to either the counter or the wall behind the basin. The most common undermount sinks are made of stainless steel.

LEFT White apron sinks with bridge-style faucets complement tan concrete counters and a subway-tile backsplash in this minimalist kitchen. They also establish work zones. Flanking the centered stove—one paired with a microwave and the other with a dishwasher—they allow one person to cook while another cleans up. A pot filler on the stove further lightens the sinks' workload.

TOP RIGHT A drop-in stainless-steel sink with an extending spray nozzle is a hardworking addition to a large central island. The vast granite counter offers plenty of room for drying pots and pans or preparing a meal.

BOTTOM LEFT Mounting this bridge-style faucet to the stone backsplash left plenty of room for a large single-basin undermount sink.

BOTTOM RIGHT An integrated sink and backsplash, cast from the same material as the counters, create a streamlined look in a kitchen with many different materials and textures.

INTEGRATED sinks are cast or constructed of the same material as the countertop and fused to it, so there is effectively no seam or separation. The basin is simply a continuation of the countertop, making cleanup and maintenance simple. It's also an approach favored by people who like to keep the total number of surfaces and materials to a minimum. Integrated sinks can be fabricated of stone, solid surfacing, concrete, or stainless steel. A backsplash and grooved drainboard can also be integrated into the sink, making the entire area easy to wipe down.

APRON sinks, also known as farmhouse sinks, are basins set into a hole cut into the front edge of the counter, with the front of the sink exposed. The most common examples are the classic soapstone sink and the extremely popular white porcelain version, but apron sinks are now available in just about any material, including steel, copper, and aluminum. Since the basin extends past the edge of the counter, an apron sink lets you have maximum sink space. These sinks can be quite heavy, so be sure your cabinetry can take the load, especially when combined with weighty counters.

Size and Style

The first thing to think about when buying a sink is whether you want a large single basin or a sink that's divided into two or more bowls. A divided sink may have one large, deep bowl for washing dishes and another small, shallow one for rinsing vegetables or draining pasta. Or it might be equally divided into two deeper bowls. You might go with a large single bowl for the main sink if you'll have a separate prep sink for other tasks. If you'll have only one sink, you'll probably want multiple bowls. With any sink, make sure the combination of sink depth and faucet height will accommodate your largest pots and pans.

An attached or adjacent drainboard allows you to set rinsed dishes or a strainer of vegetables out of the way of the faucet without a puddle of water. Drop-in and undermount sinks are both available with drainboards built in, but an integrated or apron sink offers the chance to incorporate a drainboard into the countertop.

When it comes to style of sinks, function should take priority over looks. It's true that stainless-steel sinks and industrial-style faucets lend themselves to contemporary kitchens, while apron sinks and bridge faucets make the most sense in a traditional kitchen. But it's not uncommon to see a steel sink in a cottage kitchen or an apron sink in a loft, so be sure to focus on what matches your washing-up preferences.

Assets and Maintenance

The various sink materials have just a few relative strengths and issues to consider. Keep in mind that whichever sink you decide on, it's a good idea to run water through the drain before it's installed. You want to know before it's mounted, along with the counter and the faucet, if it doesn't drain properly.

LEFT The classic look of a white apron sink goes perfectly with wooden counters and traditional framed cabinets. A deep, single-basin apron sink and a gooseneck chrome faucet can accommodate large jobs for both cooking and washing up.

OPPOSITE PAGE, TOP A deep double-basin sink with a sprayer attachment is ideal for a kitchen with only one sink, as it's large enough to serve as a prep area and dishwashing station at the same time.

ENAMELED CAST IRON comes in a range of colors, is extremely durable and heavy, and should be caulked well at the seam to prevent water from rusting the underside.

SOAPSTONE AND SLATE are relatively porous, so they need to be sealed just like a countertop of the same material.

SOLID-SURFACE materials are the most affordable option for integrated sinks, but they shouldn't come into contact with a scalding-hot pot.

COPPER weathers to what many people consider a beautiful green patina. Preserving the shiny copper finish requires routine polishing.

STAINLESS STEEL is sold in a range of gauges, or thicknesses, with lower numbers indicating thicker metal. An 18-gauge sink is good and strong, while a 22-gauge product will be easily dented. Stainless steel also comes in various finishes, from mirrored to matte. Brushed or matte finishes are better at hiding fingerprints and water spots and are easier to maintain. Only chrome-nickel blends are truly "stainless."

Save a Sink

The greenest solution will always be to consume less, either by keeping what you have or making use of something that already exists. Where sinks are concerned, recycled options exist—such as the recycled aluminum sink at right—but consider the benefits of salvage. Many of today's most popular sink styles are reproductions of sinks that are still around. Rescue one from a junkyard or salvage shop and you'll not only save a sink—and possibly some cash—but you'll ratchet up the character of your kitchen. Plus, old sinks often make better design sense. Architect Kathryn Rogers recently used a cast-iron sink like the one at upper right, which is actually a complete countertop with integrated sink, drainboard, and backsplash. "That's something I will do a lot more of," she says. "It's so practical!"

LEFT This aluminum apron sink is handsome, relatively lightweight, and recycled.

RIGHT Cast-iron integrated sinks like this one are available as reproductions, but the originals can still be found secondhand.

BELOW Vintage sinks come in all shapes, sizes, colors, and materials and add tremendous personality to a kitchen.

Faucets

The latest restaurant element to be adapted for the home chef is the industrial sprayer with coiled hose.

TOP Antique styling, like the curved neck of this deck-mounted bridge faucet, and brushed nickel finishes are becoming increasingly popular in kitchen design. This set comes complete with an antique-style sprayer and soap dispenser.

BOTTOM LEFT Pull-out sprayers are handy and require one less hole in your counter, which is important if you include a purified-water tap and soap dispenser, as shown in this photo.

BOTTOM RIGHT Pot fillers are all the rage in kitchen remodels. It's possible to run the water line up in front of the wall and then hide it behind a backsplash.

The material options for faucets are slimmer than most other kitchen choices. Metal finishes are the most popular, with brass fittings and ceramic handles making a comeback in recent years, but with a little searching you can find a faucet to match almost any style and color of your kitchen. Beyond style, your choice of faucet will be dictated by two things: whether it will mount to the sink, the counter, or the wall; and how many holes it fits into. If you buy a sink with predrilled holes, you'll need a faucet that matches up with them.

Faucet Types

Faucets can be grouped into three basic categories:
CENTER-SET faucets fit into a single hole and have either a single lever for water control or separate hot and cold handles that branch off the spigot.
SPREAD-FIT faucets take three holes: for the hot handle, the spigot, and the cold handle. The hot and cold holes are spaced either 4 or 8 inches apart.
BRIDGE faucets fit into two holes: one for the hot handle and one for the cold. The connection that runs between the two (and feeds the water up the spigot) sits above the counter.

All three faucet types are available in a range of styles and mounting options. Faucets can be jointed, swiveling, or fixed in place. Goosenecks and other tall faucets make room for large pots. And then there's the sprayer, which is especially important if you go with a fixed faucet. Traditionally a separate element requiring another hole, extendable sprayers are now featured on many faucets.

Experts warn that an inexpensive faucet could actually cost you more in the long run. Well-made faucets have solid brass workings and ceramic-disc valves that fit to perfection and stand up to daily wear. Lesser faucets are widely available, but Brian Eby points out that the cost of a plumber's visit to fix a leaky faucet could have paid for a better faucet to begin with. However, Kevin Price notes that there are also overpriced fixtures on the market. His advice is to pick a fixture you like, check that its fittings are brass and ceramic, and then run it past your plumber before buying it.

Specialty Items

Cropping up behind sinks everywhere are purified-water taps. Usually these are short, slender gooseneck spigots with hot and cold levers. Another popular little spout is the built-in soap dispenser. It doesn't require any plumbing, of course, but it typically matches the faucet. Both require additional holes in your countertop. If you incorporate them, you might go with a center-set faucet to avoid a forest of fixtures behind your sink.

A major faucet trend is the pot filler—a jointed spigot mounted to the wall behind the stove—which allows you to fill a large pot with water without hauling it from the sink to the stove. It requires extra plumbing, but many people find it a worthwhile feature.

At the heart of this unfitted kitchen is a pair of mismatched apron-front sinks, one in soapstone and the other in porcelain. Though both are brand new, they look as if they could have been salvaged from the space before it was remodeled.

For the owner of this New Hampshire home, which dates to 1720, it was critical that the brand-new kitchen not look brand new. Changes were made to the awkward space—an addition from the 1970s—that included altering the ceiling height and adding a small bump-out to make room for a dining table. Then, working with interior designer and architect Benjamin Nutter, the owner pulled together an unfitted kitchen that looks as if it evolved over decades, if not longer. The unfitted philosophy was applied to every last detail, including the sinks.

The Elements

- **Sinks:** Soapstone single-basin sink; white porcelain prep sink

- **Counters:** White marble and edge-grain butcher block

- **Backsplash:** White subway tile; full wall behind range

- **Cabinets:** White-painted face-frame cabinets with brown-painted, hutch-style upper; flush-mounted drawers with bead detail and frame-and-panel doors; "leg" detailing

- **Island:** Walnut-stained cabinetry, slightly mismatched to perimeter cabinets

- **Hardware:** Brushed nickel bin pulls and knobs; blackened bronze on island

- **Additional Storage:** Freestanding hutch; wall-mounted plate rack; walk-in pantry

- **Appliances:** Black professional-grade range with custom hood; paneled refrigerator and dishwasher drawers; stainless-steel combination oven

- **Flooring:** Stained hardwood in diamond pattern

- **Seating:** Farmhouse table and Shaker chairs

- **Finishing Touches:** Yellow walls; high round window; exposed ceiling beams; transferware platters as wall art; red and green dishware in open display

Q+A: Benjamin Nutter and his colleague Rick Bernard talk about creating a new kitchen that appears to have been there all along.

Though it is new, this kitchen really looks like it's from another era, particularly with its unfitted style. The mismatched sinks are a big part of that. Was that specifically your aim?
We give the homeowner a lot of credit for that. She had images that appealed to her, and she was after this notion that it wouldn't look like a brand-new kitchen but rather one that had been improved over time. The fact that the sinks didn't match was definitely part of what she was looking to achieve.

Are both sinks new?
They are both new, yes. The big one is Boston soapstone, and the little one is from Kohler.

Can you talk about some of the other elements that contribute to the look your client was after?
The range is Viking, but the hood was custom-made to match it. There were a few stock options, but the client, Maria, didn't like any of them. She had pictures of some with a similar shape (to the final hood), and we added some details and then finished it to match the range. The plate rack is another detail that would appear to be a piece they found in a secondhand shop, but it was detailed and made by the cabinetmaker. Another example is the cabinet, where the upper row of drawers juts out with little brackets. You get the sense that it could have been in a doctor's office or something, brought in and retrofitted for use in this kitchen. It's a nice detail and a good example of a deeper counter allowing the refrigerator to feel more natural in the space.

The subway tile was chosen because it's so classic, but the owners also live in New York City and have this country farmhouse in New Hampshire. So it's something they've seen in New York, and they recognize its classic character.

Maria basically used fairly traditional, classic elements. The floor is maple, but then she did that really neat pattern on it, for instance. It's interesting how all of those individual elements came together so well.

So you have the plate rack and the one hutch-style upper. Is that all there is in the way of upper storage?
Yes, which is why the pantry space was important to them, because it wasn't feasible to introduce more upper storage into the kitchen. With the appliance locations and the little eating nook at the end, there's very little wall surface where you could introduce it. And Maria knew she wanted a spot for the free-standing piece. The pantry is an old walk-in, below-ground root cellar, so it was waterproofed over the top, and cabinetry was introduced into it for food and wine storage. It's not enormous, but it's convenient to the kitchen and really augments the storage space.

What else is there about this project that you're particularly pleased with?
The space faces north, so the wall color, the windows, and that extra little round window really help bring a sense of daylight in. The clients had a very good interior designer who really got what Maria was looking for, and we're very happy with the results.

THIS PAGE Beside the small sink, the single hutch upper and built-in refrigerator were painted the same color and treated with crown molding.

OPPOSITE PAGE, TOP Just down the hall from the kitchen, the original cellar is now a pantry and wine cellar.

OPPOSITE PAGE, MIDDLE The faucet, with its top-mount soap basket, evokes an earlier era as well.

OPPOSITE PAGE, BOTTOM The hood was custom-designed to work with but not exactly match the range. The plate rack is also new. The wall is covered in white subway tile.

THIS PAGE The cleanup zone, with primary sink, dishwasher, and dish storage, is just inside the kitchen doorway. Opposite the range are open counter space and Schwartz's prep sink (see page 98).

OPPOSITE PAGE, TOP Schwartz originally planned for a big kitchen in what became the dining space. He's now happy with the efficiency of the smaller kitchen.

OPPOSITE PAGE, BOTTOM Unable to find exactly what he wanted, Schwartz commissioned the big stainless-steel sink from a restaurant-supply company and has since had it copied for clients.

The efficiency of a small kitchen hinges entirely on how well the space is planned. Architect Neal Schwartz says his small kitchen works because in his house "there's a strict division of labor. One person likes to cook, and one person likes to clean up." So he used sinks to establish zones. He clustered the main sink, dishwasher, and dish storage together at one end, which means there's no need for his partner to cross into the cooking zone. Likewise, the cooking zone has a prep sink to keep Schwartz out of the cleanup zone. Barstools outside a half-wall keep guests out of the kitchen entirely.

The Elements

- **Sinks:** Stainless-steel undermount primary and prep sinks; primary sink with built-in drain-board; prep sink with pot-filler faucet and foot pedals

- **Cabinets:** Custom frameless mahogany cabinets; single floating upper cabinet with back-painted glass front

- **Additional Storage:** Recessed pottery niche; trio of short floating shelves; pantry cabinet

- **Hardware:** Steel pulls

- **Counters:** Pietra Cardosa

- **Backsplash:** Full wall of back-painted glass with stainless-steel strip along counter

- **Appliances:** Stainless-steel refrigerator, range, hood, and dishwasher drawers

- **Flooring:** Jarrah wood

- **Seating:** Classic Bertoia barstools

- **Finishing Touches:** Square picture window; recessed lights

"I don't think I would ever use hand-operated sinks for myself again! The foot pedal means you always have your hands free and can control the water directly as you need it. It took about two seconds to get used to. In fact, I find myself tapping my foot at the big sink, looking for the controls."

—Architect Neal Schwartz

THIS PAGE This pantry closet—at the right end of the kitchen, with direct access from the dining room—creates a third zone. It houses the toaster, coffeemaker, microwave, and other supplies.

OPPOSITE PAGE The prep sink has a jointed pot filler for a faucet, which is operated by foot pedals, like a surgical sink. Schwartz also found a Japanese cutting board that fits perfectly over the sink, giving him additional workspace. He can easily slide the board out of the way or even slide scraps into the sink through one of the holes.

Chapter 5

Appliances

Without its appliances, a kitchen is just a storage room. Appliances are what enable the keeping and cooking of food—the very point of a kitchen. And the choices go well beyond the basic refrigerator and stove. Induction cooktops, convection ovens, warming drawers, and other high-tech offerings can raise the game of any home chef. The challenge is to figure out which mix of appliances will add up to exactly the right functionality for your household.

Updating your appliances with more energy-efficient models is a smart move for the environment and your budget.

Appliance Considerations

THIS PAGE Stainless-steel appliances—including a glass-front fridge, dishwasher drawers, and an oversized range and hood—are standouts in this otherwise understated kitchen.

OPPOSITE PAGE The vertical grain of the cabinetry visually heightens this kitchen, which includes a chef-worthy cooktop and double oven as well as an elegantly paneled refrigerator.

Like cabinets, countertops, and sinks, appliances are subject to changing fashions, but with appliances there's the technology factor as well. New appliances don't just look different from older ones—they are different, with new models becoming smarter and sleeker every year.

Form and Function

Today's appliances not only come in a wider range of styles than ever before, they also do more, and do it much more efficiently. Refrigerators are available in countless sizes and configurations, allowing you to pick one tailored to your space and usage. Traditional ranges are giving way to separate cooktops and wall ovens, which allow for more than one cook in the kitchen. Microwaves now serve a multitude of functions, by combining the technologies of convection as well as toaster ovens for an all-in-one speed-cooking machine.

There's no denying the influence of the restaurant kitchen on the home version. It wasn't long ago that a restaurant-style fridge was a status item. Stainless-steel appliances are now ubiquitous, and "professional-style" and commercial

Energy Issues

Updating your appliances will save money and help the environment. Government agencies have mandated increased efficiency in recent years, and the difference is remarkable: A new energy-efficient refrigerator requires half the power of a model dating to 1993. The Department of Energy (DOE) sets minimum performance levels, while the Federal Trade Commission requires the yellow EnergyGuide labels, which allow you to compare energy usage among different models. Energy Star, a joint program of the DOE and the Environmental Protection Agency, awards its seal to the best-performing products. Because it takes a better-made appliance to meet those higher standards, Energy Star products may cost more up front but will save you money over the long term in better performance and lower monthly utility bills. Many power companies also offer incentives for replacing outdated appliances with Energy Star models. Be sure to recycle or donate your old appliances.

Although Americans are switching to more efficient appliances, another trend is installing more appliances than ever. Homes might have two or more refrigerators in the kitchen and a mini-fridge in the den or backyard, plus an electric cooktop, warming drawer, trash compactor, water purifier, and always-on coffeemaker. Any savings you get from high-efficiency appliances will be offset by an increase in your total energy load, so choose your appliances wisely in their numbers as well as their specifications.

appliances are standard top-of-the-line offerings. But oversize stainless-steel appliances aren't the only trend. You'll also see the opposite: refrigerators and dishwashers that can be paneled to match your cabinets, allowing them to blend in rather than stand out. And then there's the growing prevalence of colorfully enameled retro-style and refurbished appliances.

Refrigerators

As the most frequent destination in a kitchen, a refrigerator must suit the capacity needs and traffic pattern of your household. The latest full-size models offer a variety of configurations and options in finish materials.

I used to be that the only real choice to make in buying a refrigerator was the color—maybe bubblegum pink in the 1950s and harvest gold in the '70s. But visit an appliance store today and you'll find the myriad refrigerator options jaw-dropping.

Full-Size Refrigerators

Even among full-size refrigerators there is great variety: top-mount freezers, bottom-mount freezers, side-by-sides, and even French-door styles, which have split refrigerator doors above a freezer drawer. But that's not all. What color or material would you like? With matching or contrasting handles? Solid doors or glass? Filtered water and an ice dispenser? And will that be recessed into the freezer door or mounted inside?

Dimensions are critical when you are shopping for a refrigerator. If yours will fit into an existing slot, or if you simply have a limited amount of space available, measure carefully and look for a fridge that fits. In addition to the height, width, and depth measurements, you'll also need to consider the span of the doors when they're open. For example, a narrow aisle between the fridge and an island might dictate a side-by-side because the doors are narrower and thus require less space to swing open. Pay attention to the hinge area as well, particularly if the fridge will be set into an opening or up against a wall. You don't want the adjacent surface to prohibit the door from opening or for the fridge door to damage that adjacent surface. Even if you have room for a large refrigerator, make sure it will fit through your door on delivery day.

Keep in mind that the style and configuration you select affect a refrigerator's interior space. Glass doors rule out any shelves or compartments in the inside of the doors. You won't fit a large pizza into the freezer half of a

When truly built in, refrigerators are not just cabinet depth but are paneled to match your cabinets and have matching pulls.

standard side-by-side, for instance, nor a party tray into the fridge. French-door units are available with split or full-width shelves, but some also have full-width drawers, requiring that you open both doors in order to open the drawers. When considering any fridge, look for adjustable shelves and multiple drawers with individual humidity controls.

If your refrigerator will be freestanding, as opposed to tucked into the

cabinetry or a niche of some sort, be aware that not all are designed to be seen from the side. If you shop from photos—online or by catalog—and see only the front of the unit, read the description carefully. You might think you're buying an entirely stainless-steel fridge, only to find that the cabinet—the sides and top—is black or gray.

Mini-Fridges and Wine Coolers

Once reserved for dorm rooms and wet bars, undercounter refrigerators are gaining favor as adjuncts to full-size units. Today they can be purchased with or without freezer compartments and are most often used for snacks and beverages. Putting one in a family room, guest suite, media room, or outdoor living space can save trips to the kitchen. And strategically adding one in the kitchen—perhaps on the outer side of an island—can help keep people out of the central work zone.

A specialty version of the mini-fridge is the wine cooler, which has rows of pullout racks for storing wine bottles on their sides. Wine is best kept at consistent temperatures, ideally lower than average room temperature, and wine coolers enable that. Many have multiple temperature zones, since whites and sparkling wines are typically stored and served at lower temperatures than red wines. If you're a connoisseur of fine wines and like to keep older vintages on hand, a wine cooler may be worth the investment. (If you drink younger or less expensive wines and don't store them long term, you might opt for a standard wine rack or the built-in slots in your full-size refrigerator. See page 168.) Wine coolers are available in full-height units as well as undercounter versions.

Another product you'll find alongside mini-fridges is the undercounter ice maker. These tend to look like even narrower mini-fridges, with the door opening to an ice compartment. A water line is required to run an ice maker.

Refrigerator Drawers

The latest development in refrigerators is the refrigerated drawer. Designed to stack and sized so that a pair fits neatly under a counter, refrigerated drawers were initially adopted by people wanting additional refrigerated storage but not a

FAR LEFT A charming red mini-fridge full of beverages, tucked into a simple niche with a countertop, is like a beacon to the thirsty.

ABOVE LEFT Available in many sizes, wine fridges have become as ubiquitous as coffee makers.

ABOVE This wine cooler tops a pair of freezer drawers just like the refrigerator to its left. All are paneled to match the cabinetry, resulting in a colorful, clean-lined space. The beamed ceiling adds warmth and character to this unique kitchen.

ABOVE RIGHT For this small summer-home kitchen, three refrigerator drawers and one freezer drawer replaced an overbearing full-size fridge. In stainless steel, they blend right in with the steel cabinets.

second fridge. With so many open kitchens and with home-owners wanting fridges to be as minimalist as possible, more and more people are forgoing the full-size fridge entirely and choosing multiple drawers, often locating them in an island. Drawers are also ideal for smaller kitchens or second homes, where capacity requirements aren't as large. Refrigerator drawers are also popular for use as a child-height snack station that lets kids easily help themselves.

ARCHITECT
KATHRYN ROGERS ON

The Price of Stainless

Stainless-steel appliances may be ubiquitous now, but they still cost more than standard white. If going with stainless means you'll have to skimp on something else in your kitchen remodel, Kathryn Rogers advises not to do it. "Buy better cabinets," she says. "Spend money doing the permanent things well—things like the layout and the windows. You can always upgrade your appliances later."

Ranges, Cooktops, Ovens

G as or electric? Four burners or six? One oven chamber or two? A combined unit or separate cooktop and wall oven (or ovens)? These are just a few of the questions you'll face as you shop for a cooking appliance—the kitchen's engine.

Ranges

Traditionally, the standard range was 30 inches wide, combined four burners and an oven, and was available as a slide-in unit (designed to be flanked by cabinets) or drop-in style (sitting not just between cabinets but on a low cabinet base). It usually had a storage or broiling drawer. These days, the options, price points, colors, and alternatives branch out widely from there. If you have multiple cooks in your kitchen or you often cook for large groups, you might want a 48- or 60-inch range, with six or eight burners, a grill or griddle, and multiple oven chambers. The consensus is still that gas is optimal for stovetop cooking, offering instant on and off and precision control of the visible flame, while electric, with its steadier temperature and self-cleaning capacity, is best for the oven. Dual-fuel ranges allow that combination. A good range, with well-crafted controls and sturdy grills and racks, can last 15 years, so think of it as an investment.

Interest in commercial and professional-style ranges is on the rise. What's the difference? Commercial ranges—those made for restaurant kitchens—cook at higher temperatures than residential ranges (15,000 or more BTUs versus 10,000 or less), allowing not just faster boiling but quicker searing of meats and other techniques professionals rely on. These ranges are deeper, their pilot lights are always on, and they aren't insulated, so they require at least 3 inches of clearance on each side. Professional-style ranges offered by the manufacturers of residential lines have the look and firepower of commercial ranges but with the safety features, insulation, and self-cleaning mechanisms of their other models, so they often cost more. Not every range that looks like a commercial range cooks like one—check the BTU rating. And if you consider a commercial range, check local ordinances and your insurance policy for potential prohibitions.

Other popular range options include enamel-finished vintage styles, whether refurbished older stoves or new ones designed to look like those of another era. A refurbished stove brings character to a kitchen—as well as authenticity, if you're doing a historical renovation—and it also keeps a stove out of the landfill. And older stoves can have sensible features like multiple smaller oven chambers or flip-up burner covers. Retro-style new ranges also come in a wide variety of lively colors not otherwise available.

OPPOSITE PAGE Amid pops of primary colors, a fire-engine red professional gas range is the perfect focal point at the end of the galley.

ABOVE A professional-grade range can look at home in a charming old-fashioned kitchen.

RIGHT The six-burner, double-oven, professional-strength range has become a new standard of excellence.

BELOW A vintage stove, whether one powered by gas or a true antique that can be wood-fired, may need to be serviced more often than a modern model.

Cooktops

Separate cooktops and wall ovens continue to be popular, largely because a cooktop is easy to locate in an island or a peninsula and because separating them allows one person to use the stove while another uses the oven, without getting in each other's way. If you have multiple cooks in your household, or if you want multiple oven chambers but don't have the floor space for a range big enough to hold them, separate appliances might be the best approach.

The flexibility afforded by a cooktop goes beyond location. Like a range, a cooktop can be gas or electric. Electric options include traditional coils or a glass-ceramic "smooth top" (with warning lights that remain on until the burners have cooled). Induction cooktops are another option. These heat up special cookware electromagnetically, are extremely energy efficient, and rival gas in the level of temperature control, but they're more expensive. Many cooktops offer modular units for infinite customization, including dual-fuel options. You might include a grill, griddle, wok, steamer, or deep fryer along with standard gas, electric, or induction stovetop elements.

Hoods and Other Ventilation

Whether you choose a range or a cooktop, you'll need to vent it—preferably directing heat, moisture, odors, and carbon monoxide to the outdoors

ABOVE LEFT Apron-front cooktops have knobs on the front rather than on the cooking surface. Look for continuous grates, which allow pots to slide smoothly from one burner to the other (or straddle two). Here, the tapered white hood above black cabinetry is dramatic but not overpowering.

ABOVE RIGHT This cooktop combines gas and electric elements and sits directly above a wall oven.

through a duct rather than simply recirculating them with a fan. Restaurant-style chimney hoods are quite popular, but cabinet undermount ventilation is still widely available, as are hood liners that install into a housing designed to match your cabinets. If you locate your stove or cooktop in an island rather than against an outside wall, venting it may require a separate kitchen exhaust system. Downdraft vents, which pop up or are mounted behind the burners rather than above them, pull grease and odors from the surface but are generally less effective than overhead styles, particularly at capturing smoke. Commercial hoods are not recommended, as they are extremely powerful and—especially in a well-sealed newer home—can

cause backdrafting, pulling exterior air, debris, and contaminants down through your chimney or other structural openings.

When shopping for ventilation, consider how much noise it puts out, whether it has an exterior or an interior blower, and how powerful it is. The ratings for hoods are given in CFMs, or cubic feet of air moved per minute. You'll need a hood sized and rated to match your stove's heating capacity, but ideally not less than 250 CFM. It's possible for even a large and impressive-looking hood to run at less than 200 CFM, so don't assume size equals power.

ABOVE LEFT An ivory hood strikes an old-fashioned note above the modern range in this country-eclectic kitchen.

ABOVE RIGHT This six-burner gas cooktop requires a powerful hood, such as this stainless model chosen to accentuate the streamlined drawer pulls and the trim on the frosted glass cabinets.

Wall Ovens

As with cooktops, wall ovens can be easier to work into a floor plan than a range—especially if you want more than one, because they can be stacked. Wall ovens are built in and can be positioned at any height, so you'll find them solo or side by side in base cabinets or stacked into full-height units or walls. If you situate one just above waist level, you won't have to squat to check progress or to maneuver cookware in and out. As with ranges, wall ovens can be gas or electric, thermal or convection. Traditional thermal ovens use radiant heat from heating elements to cook the food, while convection ovens circulate warm air around the food for faster and more even cooking. Many ovens offer both options. You'll also find convection steam ovens that counter the drying effects of traditional convection cooking.

Microwaves and Small Ovens

Microwaves use radio-wave technology to cook food much more quickly than thermal ovens can, but you can't brown with them. So they're used mainly for defrosting and reheating and for cooking select foods. Toaster ovens are small electric ovens that work exactly like their larger counterparts but also offer toast settings. And small convection ovens are popular adjuncts to full-size ovens. You can now buy all of these smaller ovens in various combinations, such as microwave-convection ovens and convection-toaster ovens. Many are meant to be built in, but because their dimensions vary greatly and because they may be replaced more often than larger ovens, give some thought to whether building them in makes sense. Whether built in or sitting on a counter, they are best located between waist and shoulder height.

Warming Drawers

A warming drawer is just what it sounds like: a drawer, built into your cabinetry, that keeps food warm in the event it finishes cooking before you can serve it. Particularly helpful for serving large meals all at once, some models also offer humidity controls to keep food moist. Locating a warming drawer across from or directly below your oven makes it easy for you to transfer foods from one to the other.

TOP LEFT Wall ovens are available in mix-and-match units sized to stack. In this set, the microwave is housed in a surround that makes it the same width as the oven and the warming drawer below.

TOP RIGHT Microwaves tend to be replaced more often than ovens, so you might consider sliding one into a niche rather than building it in. This one is at counter level so kids can make easy use of it.

LEFT Situating a pair of warming drawers side by side consolidates heat. The apron-front cooktop above features continuous grates and a griddle.

This double oven is conveniently located near a warming drawer, above which is a built-in espresso maker.

When it comes to cleanup, there are two appliances you may wish to have near your sink: a dishwasher (or two) for helping manage the dirty dishes, and a trash compactor for discarding any nonrecyclable waste.

Dishwashers

Like refrigerators, dishwashers are now available in drawer form. Drawers have the advantage of running separately, so you can feel good about washing just one drawer's worth of dishes. Many models can be paneled to match your cabinetry and offer controls that are inside the top of the door rather than on the outside, making for a cleaner façade.

Dishwasher technology is ever changing, but the best models are water and energy efficient, run quietly, and have a range of sensors and cycles to choose from. Many Energy Star models allow you to turn down your water heater because they have internal booster heaters that heat the water as it's used. Additional cycle options boost the price of the machine, so buy one that has just what you need and no more.

Because dishwashers are always built in, the standard size (approximately 24 inches wide) has remained steady, but there are European models that diverge from that width. So make sure to check the measurements of both the slot and the model you choose to slide into it.

Trash Compactors

With the prevalence of curbside recycling and the corresponding reduction in garbage, the interest in trash compactors has decreased in recent years. But if you live in a high-rise or are charged by the bag for garbage collection, you may still appreciate a compactor, which can compress four bags of trash into one. Locate your compactor on the opposite side of the sink from your dishwasher. When shopping for one, check its noise levels, odor controls, and safety features.

OPPOSITE PAGE Conveniently located next to the dishwasher drawers, this trash compactor makes loading the dishes a one-stop process.

RIGHT Dishwasher drawers, like these in stainless steel, allow you to wash a single drawer at a time, conserving water and energy.

BELOW Dishwashers with customizable front panels and controls hidden inside the top of the door can virtually disappear into the surrounding cabinetry.

ARCHITECT
BILL INGRAM ON

Appliance Placement

Bill Ingram believes that placement is more important than style when it comes to appliances. "Poor placement can really wreck a room," he says. "But if appliances are the right depth and proportion for the space, and sensibly located, they'll blend in nicely whether paneled or not."

Range of Interest

THIS PAGE The classic blue La Cornue range is the focal point of this over-sized kitchen.

OPPOSITE PAGE, TOP Everything is handcrafted here, from the island to the Swedish farm table to the "windows" above the Dutch door and storage unit.

OPPOSITE PAGE, BOTTOM The blue porcelain knobs are a perfect match with the range. The marble counters are also blue.

For the owner of this kitchen, which is scaled to host a crowd, it all began with France's iconic blue restaurant range. A patterned tile surround amplifies the range's prominence—as does the rail hung with glistening copper pots—while two dishwashers, four refrigerator drawers, and two freezer drawers literally disappear into the woodwork. The range and its surround are then reflected in thoughtful choices throughout the space.

The Elements

- **Appliances:** French commercial range; paneled dishwashers; paneled refrigerator and freezer drawers; stainless-steel built-in microwave; built-in hood with stainless-steel liner

- **Cabinets:** Painted cherry custom face-frame cabinets with partial-overlay drawers

- **Island:** Custom-built of cherry

- **Additional Storage:** Built-in storage unit and plate rack

- **Hardware:** White porcelain knobs and pulls on perimeter cabinets; coordinating blue porcelain on island

- **Counters:** Mediterranean blue marble

- **Backsplash:** Matching marble curb on rear counter; patterned ceramic-tile range surround

- **Sinks:** White ceramic undermount sinks with contrasting faucets

- **Flooring:** Chinese marble, laid on the diagonal

- **Seating:** Custom-built table and matching benches

- **Finishing Touches:** Cream, white, and blue palette; oversized windows with leaded-glass detail; Dutch door; leaded-glass mural above storage built-in; wrought-iron corner shelves; hand-painted receptacle covers; collections of plates, ceramic canisters, and yellowware bowls

Q+A: Designer Michelle Rein talks about the art of collaboration and building her longtime client's dream kitchen.

Let's start with the range, the focal point of the room. Given its size and color, it would seem to have inspired the room's palette. Is that the case, or was it the other way around?
The range was the first thing Mary Jane (the homeowner) purchased, so it did inspire the rest. The blue enamel caught her eye.

It's interesting that other appliances in the space were paneled to disappear. Was that about letting the range have the spotlight all to itself?
That was probably the motivation. I think that blue range is almost artistic in style. It stands on its own as a very pretty piece. And at the time, I don't think companies were making dishwashers and refrigerators to rival that. Some of them are now doing that, but this was about three years ago.

I understand this kitchen was very much a collaborative effort, involving the architect, the builder, you and your partner, and the homeowner, among others. At what point did you get involved in the project?
Originally the project was being coordinated by the architect. I've known Mary Jane for about 11 years, and we'd done stained glass and furniture for her before. She wanted us to do the cabinetry, so she insisted we be pulled in. We were originally working with the architect, Philip Anosovich. We kept some of the bones Phil laid out but expanded on the architectural detail that the homeowner loves. It was easy because I knew this client so well, and then I took over as far as the interior design decisions went.

This one's been quite a bit of fun. Because I wasn't initially in charge, the kitchen ended up going in one wall at a time—first the windows, then the La Cornue, then the plate wall was designed, and then the shelving over the mezzanine last. If I had it to do again, I'd design it all first, but it's gone in pretty cohesively.

Anytime there are multiple creative people or teams working together, it can be complicated. What do you think is the key to a successful collaboration?
Our main goal is to make the homeowner happy, to know that she's enjoying the process and what we're producing. If we don't all have that in mind, it'd be silly to even try to work together. So that's the glue that holds it all together. And it helps if you are working with a good group of people. I asked a lot from everyone, and they all knocked my socks off. It takes a real group effort to turn out something special.

Of course, we all have different motivations. The builder wants to get it done in a certain time frame and budget. I want Mary Jane to be thrilled with every bit of it.

TOP LEFT A custom-built plate rack holds patterned plates, which the homeowner rotates seasonally.

BOTTOM LEFT While the range is showcased, the remaining appliances are camouflaged. The island contains a dishwasher and four refrigerator drawers. Another dishwasher and two freezer drawers occupy the rear wall with the stainless-steel microwave.

RIGHT If you can't spot the receptacle cover here, it's because it's been hand-painted to match the tile. The alcove ceiling is tiled in coordinating blue to disguise the hood liner.

Hidden Assets

Discreet appliances, smart space planning, and sophisticated materials add up to an elegant and efficient galley. The surface interest of the wall on the left balances out the visual weight of all the cabinetry on the right. A skylight brightens the space.

The words "galley kitchen" don't generally conjure up a space as glamorous as this one. It's the work of a knowledgeable homeowner who acted as her own general contractor and invested in high-quality appliances and surface materials. She opted for a separate cooktop and oven, which have less presence than a standard range, and hid the rest of the appliances, including a full-size washer and dryer, behind paneled doors. Obscuring the appliances in that way and forgoing upper cabinets on one wall resulted in a kitchen that feels much more spacious than it is, while still meeting all of the functional needs.

The Elements

- **Appliances:** Stainless-steel convection wall oven and gas cooktop with pop-up vent; paneled refrigerator and dishwasher; stackable washer and dryer

- **Cabinets:** Painted, custom, frameless base cabinets; face-frame, hutch-style uppers with rippled-glass doors

- **Additional Storage:** Laundry closet

- **Hardware:** Mission-style knobs in polished nickel and octagonal knobs in crystal; crystal doorknobs for refrigerator and washer/dryer doors

- **Counters:** Emperador Dark marble with offset edge

- **Backsplash:** Emperador Dark marble curb behind sink; opposite wall of half ivory, half polished-onyx subway tiles

- **Sink:** White porcelain single basin with exposed-bridge gooseneck faucet

- **Flooring:** Dark-stained oak

- **Finishing Touches:** White, cream, yellow, and brown palette; crown molding; vintage-style light fixtures

OPPOSITE PAGE, LEFT AND BOTTOM A washer and dryer, refrigerator with freezer drawers, and dishwasher are clustered together and hidden behind paneled doors with crystal doorknobs for pulls. The laundry closet conveniently faces the hallway to the bedrooms.

OPPOSITE PAGE, TOP The cooktop's pop-up vent requires an extra-deep counter. In its lowered position, it sits behind the base cabinets.

THIS PAGE Working with a smaller space often allows for more luxurious materials. Here, simple ivory subway tile is combined with polished onyx and marble. Onyx trim tile forms a border between the two wall tiles.

Chapter 6

Flooring

A good kitchen floor should be beautiful, durable, slip resistant, and watertight, but most of all it should be easy to clean. Fortunately, there are numerous flooring materials on the market that meet all of the above criteria, so you're sure to find a floor that will satisfy your taste and budget. There are bound to be messes and spills in a kitchen, so practicality and quality should be high on your list of priorities.

Rustic and imperfect, slate floor tiles come in a variety of rectangular shapes and colors—from purples and ambers to dark gray, depending on the stone's elemental makeup.

Flooring Choices

THIS PAGE Vinyl and linoleum tiles come in a variety of shapes and colors, offering endless ideas for creative applications, like this hexagonal pattern of multi-colored tiles.

OPPOSITE PAGE, CLOCKWISE FROM LEFT Standard 12-inch square linoleum tiles can be laid to create complex or simple checkerboard patterns or even stripes.

A kitchen floor is one of the more abused surfaces in any home. It must stand up to heavy foot traffic, falling objects, and constant cleaning. But it also sets a stage for your counters, cabinets, and furnishings. Whichever material you chose, keep in mind that dark, speckled, or patterned products will hide dirt and wear better than light or solid-colored varieties.

Vinyl

Readily available, easy to install, able to cover many kinds of existing floors, and made in a wide range of colors and patterns, vinyl is also the least expensive kitchen flooring option. Vinyl comes in both tile and sheet form. Some sheet vinyl has a cushioned backing, which increases both its resilience and sound absorption. Most sheet vinyl and some tiles are meant to be glued to the sub-floor, but peel-and-stick tiles are also available and are popular with do-it-yourselfers. Remember that seams are vulnerable to water, so tiles should be laid as tightly together as possible. Sheets come in rolls up to 12 feet wide, so it's possible to have a floor made from one seamless piece. The least expensive products are surface printed; they may yellow, fade, or possibly curl up at the edges over time. More expensive varieties have through-body color and are more durable.

Linoleum

Invented in 1863 and used in kitchens ever since, linoleum fell out of favor with the introduction of vinyl flooring in the mid-20th century because it required waxing, whereas vinyl floors did not. But modern linoleum flooring is as low maintenance as vinyl. Linoleum is also vastly more durable than tile—expect a floor to last 40 years—and is an eco-friendly and sustainable product that combines linseed oil with wood products and pigment on a jute backing. Linoleum is available in a wide array of colors and patterns, in sheet and tile versions, and in click-together, plank-style "floating" floors (they don't attach to the subfloor) that are suitable for do-it-yourselfers. Linoleum is naturally antibacterial, antistatic, and nontoxic, and it can be installed over some types of existing floors. Kevin Price says that linoleum can cost as much as basic hardwood, but he favors it for renovations of older homes because of its historic character.

Laminate

Laminate flooring is essentially a photograph of another surface—most often wood or stone—adhered to a pressed-wood substrate and sealed in resin. Wood-look varieties come in plank form, others in tile form. They may be glued to the floor or snapped together; the latter float over the subfloor and can be installed by handy homeowners. High-quality laminate products are more resistant to denting, scratching, and water damage at the seams than cheaper varieties. Laminate floors, particularly the floating form, can have a hollow sound when walked on unless they have a proper underlayment, in which case they are as quiet and sound absorbing as other resilient floors, such as vinyl, linoleum, and cork. Though they may look like wood or stone—particularly the high-end embossed versions—they don't have the variation or surface character of natural products. Unlike wood, laminate floors cannot be refinished.

Wood

There are two kinds of wood floors: solid wood and engineered wood, which consists of a hardwood wear layer, or veneer, adhered to pine or plywood. Beyond their natural beauty, both types of floors are eco-friendly options when all of the wood materials are certified by the Forest Stewardship Council (FSC). Even better for the environment are floorboards salvaged from older buildings or freshly milled from salvaged posts or beams. Solid wood floors should be installed by professionals, while engineered products are available as click-together floating floors that can be installed by do-it-yourselfers. Many wood flooring products are also now presealed, so there's no need for polyurethane to be applied in your home. Keep in mind that moisture causes wood to expand and warp, which can create gaps at the seams and leave the subfloor susceptible to damage. Wood will also show wear. Softer woods such as fir and pine are easier to scrape and dent than harder oak and maple, but any solid wood floor can be refinished. The ability to refinish an engineered-wood floor is limited by the thickness of the hardwood wear layer.

LEFT Wood-look laminate floors, also known as "faux wood," consist of a photo of wood laminated to a substrate.

OPPOSITE PAGE, TOP LEFT Salvaged wide-plank walnut flooring and FSC-certified cherry cabinets are paired with a recycled glass countertop and backsplash in this eco-conscious kitchen.

OPPOSITE PAGE, BOTTOM A deep cherry finish on a hardwood floor warms up an otherwise cool country-style kitchen.

OPPOSITE PAGE, TOP RIGHT End-grain hardwood floors are another way to use reclaimed wood. While the material itself is highly durable, the installation is a complex process similar to securing tiles with grout.

ARCHITECT
KATHRYN ROGERS ON

Wood Subfloors

Kathryn Rogers often removes the top layer of flooring and refinishes the Douglas fir subfloors common in older homes in her area. "The fir looks great, and it's already there! Plus, the warmth of it balances out all the stainless-steel appliances people are choosing."

Cork and Bamboo

Two of the current trends in flooring are also the most environmentally friendly. Cork flooring comes from the bark of a Mediterranean oak tree that regenerates in less than 10 years. Bamboo flooring is made from particular varieties of Asian timber bamboo—an invasive, fast-growing grass—that is split, flattened, and laminated in layers or onto a pine or plywood substrate. Cork is available as tiles and planks, while bamboo is sold in plank form. Both are available

in floating-floor and presealed varieties. Cork is extremely soft and sound absorbent and comes in a range of hues, from honey to walnut to bright colors. It can be scratched or dented more easily than hardwood. Depending on the manufacturing process used, bamboo can be more durable than many hardwoods. Once available only in natural (blond) and a slightly darker carbonized version, bamboo is now available in a range of vivid stains.

ABOVE LEFT A great choice for a kitchen where you might be on your feet for an entire day, spongy cork floor tiles have a naturally variegated pattern, so they are also great for hiding the daily debris of a high-traffic area.

ABOVE RIGHT The bamboo used for this highly durable floor is FSC certified and plantation grown (without chemicals or pesticides) and reaches maturity in just five years.

Concrete

Extremely durable and versatile, poured concrete can be tinted, stained, etched, or even embedded with just about anything that doesn't pose a tripping hazard. Concrete is a nonresilient surface, meaning it is extremely hard and reflects noise. Almost nothing you drop on it will dent or mar the surface, but a dropped glass is pretty much guaranteed to break. It is also a cool surface, which is considered a benefit in warm climates, and it's the ideal material for embedding with a radiant heating system. Poured concrete should be installed by professionals, requires sealing, and is prone to hairline cracks. It takes more than a week to cure, so build that into your schedule. Concrete is also available as tile in a range of colors.

ABOVE LEFT Humble concrete tiles inlaid with strips of dark hardwood add up to a surprisingly elegant kitchen floor.

ABOVE RIGHT By leaving the concrete slab foundation exposed, the owners of this kitchen added intrigue and limited their use of building materials.

Ceramic and Stone Tile

Experts agree that lifestyle should be the first consideration when it comes to choosing kitchen flooring. "People who have kids and dogs—especially dogs—need bulletproof flooring," says designer Michelle Rein, and that means ceramic tile. As with its use in countertops, tile has fallen out of favor in flooring, but for both stylistic versatility and durability, there's no beating tile.

Stone and ceramic tile both come in a seemingly infinite array of colors, shapes, and sizes. Grout durability and stain resistance have come a long way in recent years. Any tile rated for use on a floor will meet the basic criteria for durability and slip resistance, but not all floor tile is created equal. Glazed ceramics are impervious and wear resistant; softer, unglazed and stone tiles require sealing and are subject to wear, stains, and discoloration. The option with the highest durability and lowest maintenance requirement is porcelain tile.

Porcelain is available in a wide range of sizes, colors, textures, and shapes, including large-format tiles made to look like stone—often at a fraction of the price. "There are beautiful porcelains that are extremely durable—more durable than stone," Rein says. "Some of them have neat textures and patterns, including great nonslip surfaces, so you don't have to worry about people sliding across the floor. And you don't have to seal them." In her view, too many people automatically choose classic stone without considering the newer porcelains. If you want a floor that will look as good years down the road as it does at installation, porcelain is your best bet.

Still, many people prefer the variable textures and coloration of natural stone slabs—like marble, travertine, and slate—that ceramic tiles can't match. "Slate is a real workhorse, it looks good, and it's relatively inexpensive," says interior designer Kathy Farley. But its coarser ridges may need to be filed before sealing. In addition to the potential for higher maintenance, many stone tiles also cost more. The beauty of natural stone is unequaled—and if you're using stone counters, you may want a floor to match—but expect stone to weather and age, and plan to reseal it periodically. Also keep in mind that stone's inherent variability means yours won't precisely match the sample at the showroom.

In shopping for any tile, ask your retailer or installer about grout options, sealing requirements, and daily maintenance. Also, any coarse stone or textured ceramic will be slip resistant at any size, but smoother options like glazed ceramic or polished stone should be used in smaller sizes. The additional grout makes the surface less slippery, but you have more grout to keep sealed.

ABOVE Porcelain tile with a stone-like texture represents the best of both worlds. Here it underscores the kitchen's indoor-outdoor sensibility.

OPPOSITE PAGE, TOP LEFT Ceramic tiles are a flooring tradition that spans the globe. They come in a variety of colors and finishes as well as ready-made patterns, so creating a floor with visual interest is a cinch.

OPPOSITE PAGE, TOP RIGHT Honed and polished travertine floor tiles create a smooth, consistent backdrop that feels at home in tropical or ultra-modern settings.

OPPOSITE PAGE, BOTTOM LEFT Mosaic tiles like these, made from small squares of various neutral colored stone, are available in ready-made patterns that can be customized to fit the size and shape of your kitchen.

OPPOSITE PAGE, BOTTOM RIGHT Unglazed clay tile combines the character of stone with the economy of ceramics.

CLOCKWISE FROM LEFT
Concrete can be tinted any color of the rainbow.

Engineered wood flooring has a hardwood top layer, limiting the amount of hardwood used.

Textured stone creates a nonslip surface and hides dirt better than smooth stone, though it can be more challenging to clean.

Flooring at a glance

Vinyl

- **Assets:** Inexpensive, easy to install, available in a wide range of colors and patterns. Peel-and-stick tiles are great for do-it-yourselfers.
- **Maintenance:** Clean with a damp mop; avoid standing water at seams.
- **Price:** $
- **Green Issues:** There is a great deal of debate about potential environmental hazards related to the production and disposal of vinyl—specifically polyvinyl chloride, or PVC—so many environmentalists simply steer clear of it.

Linoleum

- **Assets:** Affordable. Resilient surface. Available in numerous colors and patterns. Extremely durable; won't scuff, scratch, or fade.
- **Maintenance:** Naturally antibacterial and antistatic; clean with a damp mop.
- **Price:** $$
- **Green Issues:** A natural product, linoleum is environmentally superior to vinyl, with which it's often confused.

Laminate

- **Assets:** Resilient; generally less expensive than genuine stone or wood; easy to install; somewhat stain resistant. Click-together versions are suitable for do-it-yourselfers.
- **Maintenance:** Clean with a damp mop and dry thoroughly. Can't be refinished.
- **Price:** $$–$$$
- **Green Issues:** The substrate may contain urea formaldehyde, and the resin may not biodegrade.

Wood

- **Assets:** Beautiful and natural; soft and sound absorbent. Floating floors are DIY friendly.
- **Maintenance:** Use a hardwood cleaner and never allow standing water.
- **Price:** $$–$$$$
- **Green Issues:** Recyclable; buy only FSC-certified products. Ask for no-added-formaldehyde engineered products, water-based stains, and nontoxic sealants.

Cork and Bamboo

- **Assets:** Natural and beautiful, available prefinished and in DIY-friendly floating-floor varieties.
- **Maintenance:** Clean with a dust cloth or damp mop and avoid standing water. Some varieties may require additional sealing.
- **Price:** $$–$$$

- **Green Issues:** The materials are green, but make sure any sealants, adhesives, and substrates are as well.

Concrete

- **Assets:** Supremely durable and versatile. Tile form may be an option for do-it-yourselfers.
- **Maintenance:** Mop clean. Must be resealed every few years.
- **Price:** $$–$$$
- **Green Issues:** Cement production is energy intensive, but fly ash can be substituted for some of the cement content, diverting the ash from the landfill. Using the house foundation as the floor decreases the amount of building materials used. Ask for nontoxic sealants or opt for wax.

Stone and Ceramic Tile

- **Assets:** Durability, versatility, and the endless color, material, and pattern options afforded by the vast array of available tiles. Ceramic tile can be suitable for do-it-yourselfers.
- **Maintenance:** Grout requires somewhat higher maintenance than tile. Stone tile requires sealing, while glazed tile is extremely low maintenance.
- **Price:** $$–$$$$
- **Green Issues:** Choose stone quarried as close to home as possible. Ceramic tile has few environmental manufacturing issues.

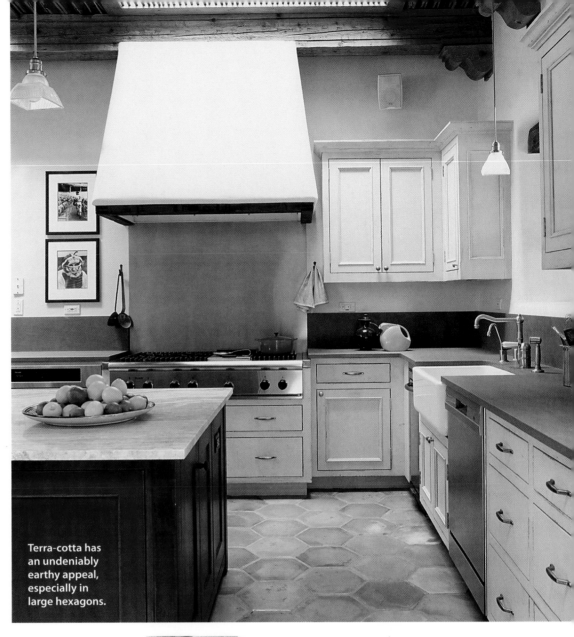

Terra-cotta has an undeniably earthy appeal, especially in large hexagons.

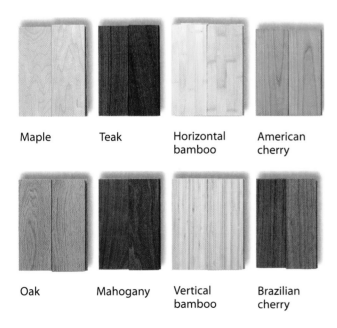

Maple

Teak

Horizontal bamboo

American cherry

Oak

Mahogany

Vertical bamboo

Brazilian cherry

Rustic hickory pecan

Fumed white oak

Cork

Case Study
Southern Sophistication

THIS PAGE A walnut travertine floor and a matching island countertop set the stage for Bill Ingram's warm and elegant Southern kitchen. Stainless-steel countertops and appliances hark back to the service kitchen the room once was.

OPPOSITE PAGE, LEFT The original brick floor in the adjacent breakfast room influenced the choice of travertine for the new kitchen floor.

OPPOSITE PAGE, RIGHT Blue plaid upholstery and brown transferware reflect the style of the kitchen.

In renovating his own Birmingham, Alabama, kitchen, architect Bill Ingram had two problems to solve: the layout and the floors. The original small service kitchen was cramped by the inclusion of a utility closet and was situated between two rooms with brick floors—one of them the breakfast room. By removing the closet, reconfiguring the doors and windows, and installing a travertine floor that complements the brick it abuts, Ingram was able to create openness and continuity.

The Elements

- **Flooring:** Walnut travertine in kitchen; brick in breakfast room

- **Cabinets:** Painted face-frame cases with partial-overlay doors and drawers in base cabinets; flush-mounted glass doors in hutch-style uppers

- **Additional Storage:** Long open shelf on brackets in front of windows; open shelves along back of island

- **Island:** Custom-built in wormy chestnut

- **Hardware:** Brass knobs throughout; keyhole detail on cabinet doors

- **Counters:** Stainless steel on both end counters, with raised edge at sink end; honed travertine on island

- **Backsplash:** Integrated stainless-steel curb

- **Sinks:** Twin integrated steel sinks; undermount steel prep sink in island

- **Appliances:** Black and stainless-steel range; stainless-steel dishwasher; commercial refrigerator with double glass doors

- **Finishing Touches:** Palette of mixed greens; painted Colonial stools with windowpane checked fabric and brass nailheads; paneled white walls; antique sconce; row of recessed lights over island; adjacent breakfast room with mix of new and antique furnishings, lantern-style light fixture

Q+A: Bill Ingram talks about choosing his floors, paying attention to detail, and the honesty of stainless-steel appliances.

How important are the floors in laying the groundwork for a design?

I think they're pretty important. I don't think there are as many choices for counters as there are for floors, so if you pick the floors first, it's easier to find other materials that work with them than if you do it the other way around.

How did you choose yours?

I knew I wanted stone because the kitchen comes off the breakfast room, which has a brick floor, and the room on the other side is also brick. I didn't want brick for the kitchen and didn't have the height to do it anyway—there was just an old vinyl floor there—so I needed something thinner, some tile, that would work with the brick on both sides of it.

What was the first design decision you made? Was there one thing you knew you wanted to do almost before you began?

The first decision was taking out the wall of the old utility room—which I relocated—and working out the layout. It's a long, narrow room, so running cabinets along the end walls and the island down the center squared it off a little bit better. I also moved a door, closed up a window, and simplified the wall spaces all the way around. There was no good clean wall anywhere.

The steel counters are unexpected in this rather Old World space and provide a nice contrast to the warmth of the floors and cabinetry. How did you decide on steel?

I knew I didn't want all the counters in stone, just the big slab on the island, so it was a process of elimination. But it

also looks like something you'd have in an old service kitchen. And it's still monolithic—it's all one piece—so it works well against the island.

Do you think stainless-steel appliances are the new white or the new harvest gold?

White. I think stainless will stay around. It has that commercial nature, and it works because it's so serviceable. Also, it's honest, not trying to be anything else. It's not decorative. It's not really trying to match anything. It just is what it is. I don't think it's a trend. I have clients who think they have to have stainless knobs and all to go with it, but I don't think so. I have brass knobs in my kitchen so it all matches the rest of the house.

You have the two hutch-style, glass-front units at one end and a long open shelf at the other—no standard upper cabinets. Is that something you're doing more of in your work?

Yes, we really always have. I just prefer it that way. I think the long cabinets get sort of heavy and they're just not that great of an idea. I really prefer open shelves whenever possible. My island is also open on one side, and all the pots and pans are there. You can just look down and find what you need—no opening doors and pulling out drawers looking for anything.

Your attention to detail is amazing—not just things like the archways for the stools or the little keyholes on the cabinet doors but the fact that you maintained absolute symmetry with the two sinks flanking the dishwasher by putting the sprayers to the outside of the

faucets. I take it there's never a point at which you think "It's just a kitchen"?

No, there's not. I'm in the kitchen a lot; it's another room of the house. I don't like to walk into a kitchen that looks like it came out of a showroom and is so foreign to the rest of the house, so I do treat kitchens like any other room.

And what about those recessed cabinets under the sinks, with the extra legroom?

You need a little more space to do that so that the cabinet is still the proper depth. You're really bringing the drawers forward, which gives you room for a deeper countertop. It's harder to make it work, but when you can, it looks really good. It breaks up that flat-front plain of cabinets and gets you away from the standard toe-kick.

Can you tell us about some of the more decorative touches—the fabrics, lights, and other accessories? Did you make those decisions early or late in the process?

They probably came later on. I pretty much knew which stools I wanted, but after I picked some of the other fabrics in the house it got me going with fabrics in the kitchen, so it all went together.

Now that it's part of your daily life, what's your favorite thing about the space?

The big work island. Everybody just gravitates to that. I can have a really nice party and have it all set up with desserts and things, and people just want to prop up on a stool and hang out all night.

Is there anything you'd do differently if you had to do it again?

I would probably do something a little different in the ceiling—maybe put a wood ceiling up there. That area of the house has a low ceiling, and I don't really mind that, but I might like to have it in wood.

TOP With the stone color picked up by the camel upholstery and the green check replaced with blue plaid, the breakfast room echoes the kitchen without matching it.

BOTTOM The stainless-steel countertop at this end of the kitchen has an integrated backsplash, twin integrated sinks, and a slightly raised front edge to contain water, creating an ideal dishwashing zone. The sensible steel also contrasts nicely with the travertine.

THIS PAGE After considering a range of options, Barr chose richly flecked brown cork tile for his renovated kitchen. It's the perfect match for his family's pottery collection and midcentury aesthetic.

OPPOSITE PAGE, LEFT The cork floor, salvaged restaurant prep table, and mahogany storage unit tie in nicely to the dining space.

OPPOSITE PAGE, RIGHT A butler's pantry was replaced with a hallway between the kitchen and the dining room. Tucked between the doorways, a storage unit houses wine bottles and drawers and doubles as a buffet. The new "butler's hall," as Barr calls it, still serves its original purpose.

Among Erik Barr's concerns in renovating his north-facing Seattle kitchen was making the most of the daylight. Opposite the existing window, he added a horizontal band of glass, which allows light to travel through the space and into the hallway beyond. He also painted the walls white. "Knowing the room was square, and not wanting to have upper cabinets, I really wanted to ground it," he says. "I wanted a dark floor but not a bottomless pit, so we narrowed it down to (flooring) that was dark but also had some visual texture"—specifically, chocolate-brown cork tile with lighter flecks. He couldn't be happier with the results.

The Elements

- **Flooring:** Cork tile; marble thresholds

- **Cabinets:** Stock frameless mahogany-veneer base cabinets

- **Additional Storage:** Matching custom mahogany wall unit; custom wine cabinet with stock fronts

- **Island:** Rolling salvaged restaurant prep table with drawers

- **Hardware:** Brushed stainless-steel bar pulls

- **Counters:** Jerusalem Gold limestone

- **Backsplash:** Matching limestone curb

- **Sink:** White porcelain apron sink

- **Appliances:** Stainless-steel refrigerator, range, and hood; paneled dishwasher designed to look like a drawer unit

- **Finishing Touches:** Orange, white, and wood palette; pottery collection; encaustic painting; reproduction George Nelson clock; recessed lights

THIS PAGE Barr chose space and light—including an interior window—rather than upper cabinets. He also eschewed L-shaped cabinets and situated the stove and fridge at opposite ends of the counter to allow plenty of workspace in between.

OPPOSITE PAGE Though the designer has a background in cabinetmaking, the mahogany-faced base cabinets (as well as the stainless-steel pulls) came from Ikea. "They've really improved in terms of quality and ingenuity. And though I may be rubbing some more brain cells together to make the measurements work, you can't beat the prices."

"I love the cork floor—absolutely love it. It's cheaper than most tile or stone and is also nice to stand on. We have a toddler, and as far as toddlers go, he's on the neat end, but we like that it's an easy cleanup." —Designer Erik Barr

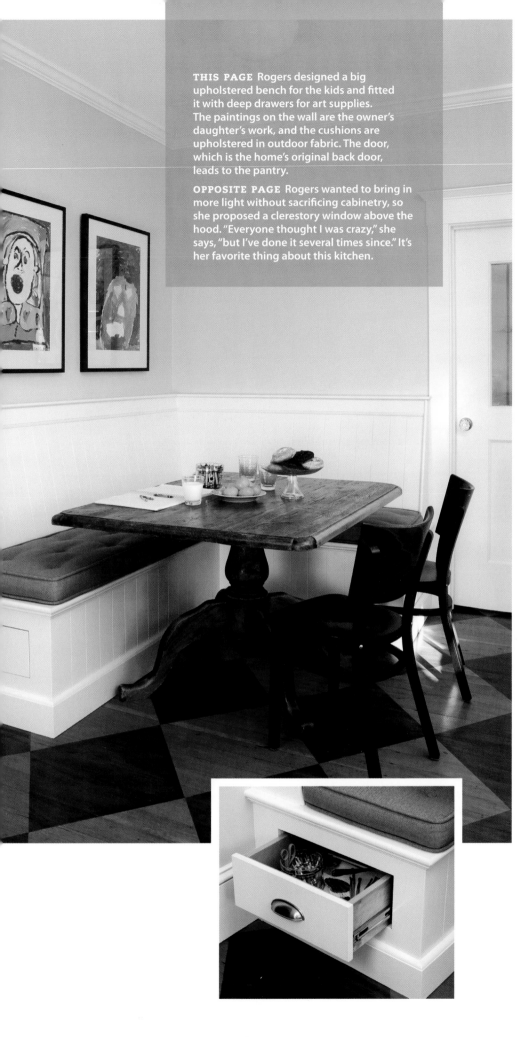

THIS PAGE Rogers designed a big upholstered bench for the kids and fitted it with deep drawers for art supplies. The paintings on the wall are the owner's daughter's work, and the cushions are upholstered in outdoor fabric. The door, which is the home's original back door, leads to the pantry.

OPPOSITE PAGE Rogers wanted to bring in more light without sacrificing cabinetry, so she proposed a clerestory window above the hood. "Everyone thought I was crazy," she says, "but I've done it several times since." It's her favorite thing about this kitchen.

Architect Kathryn Rogers is a big fan of refinishing the Douglas fir subfloors found in so many older homes, and she persuaded the owner of this kitchen to do just that. Originally envisioning a pleasant green kitchen in which to hang out with her kids, the owner ultimately agreed to white. When the custom cabinets and Calcutta marble counters were in and the work crews gone, she and her sister sat on the floor with newspaper and scissors and worked out a diamond pattern for the floor. The pattern was then scored into the floor (to prevent the black stain from bleeding) without aid of a straightedge, resulting in exactly the informal look she wanted.

The Elements

- **Flooring:** Diamond-stained Douglas fir

- **Cabinets:** Painted custom face-frame cases with flush-mounted fronts

- **Additional Storage:** Open cookbook shelf above ovens; drawers in bench; walk-in pantry with desk and laundry

- **Hardware:** Brushed nickel bin pulls and knobs

- **Counters:** Calcutta marble

- **Backsplash:** Marble curb; marble slab behind cooktop

- **Sink:** White undermount single basin

- **Appliances:** Stainless-steel cooktop, microwave, and double wall ovens; built-in hood; paneled refrigerator and dishwasher

- **Seating:** Antique table with built-in bench, paneled with beadboard and upholstered in outdoor fabric

- **Finishing Touches:** Chamois-colored walls; Dutch door; clerestory window; schoolhouse lights; built-in ceiling speakers; paintings by owner's 6-year-old daughter

THIS PAGE Apart from making a family-friendly space, the owner wanted to open up the kitchen to the garden, so Rogers put in a Dutch door and large windows that come right down to the counter. She notes that it "makes the space feel bigger because your eye goes right out the back."

OPPOSITE PAGE, TOP The custom cabinets with crown molding go all the way to the ceiling to maximize storage.

OPPOSITE PAGE, BOTTOM Though tiny, the pantry efficiently combines a writing desk, laundry machines, open shelving, and even a cubbyhole for the litter box next to the original servants' stairs.

"The owner did the floor herself after everything else was done. I love it. The warmth of it really offsets the coolness of the marble."
—Kathryn Rogers

Chapter 7

Storage and Display

Your handsome new kitchen won't make you happy unless there's a proper place to put everything, so take time to inventory your current kitchen while planning the new one. Make note of the things you don't have enough room for and items that are oversized or difficult to store. Specify what you want behind closed doors, on display, or particularly close at hand. Then map out where it all will go in the new kitchen and in what types of storage systems. The options go well beyond just cabinets or drawers.

An organized and color-coordinated kitchen can make cooking and cleanup more enjoyable. Keeping things tidy and within easy reach simplifies day-to-day tasks.

Pantries

Copious dish and wine storage and an uninterrupted counter line one wall of this multi-use galley pantry.

As kitchen walls come down and cabinetry gives way to windows, pantries are gaining in both importance and popularity. They're also being reinvented for new and varied purposes.

Butler's Pantries

It's hard to believe there was an era in which guests to a home wouldn't lay eyes on the kitchen. As designer Erik Barr describes it, "Eighty years ago the food just appeared from a room." That was due in part to the prevalence of the butler's pantry—a walk-through space that separated the kitchen and dining room in many middle- and upper-class homes. In a butler's pantry one would find dishes and glassware, serving pieces, table linens, silver, candles, and often a sink. (You can see an intact historical butler's pantry in the case study on pages 170–173.) The dining room table would have been laid with dishes from the butler's pantry, where food and drinks were also readied for presentation. And the pantry was where things were cleaned up, polished, and put away at the end of the evening.

Today the butler's pantry has reappeared in modified forms—as a dish pantry, a prep room, or a multi-use space. The mainstay is ample shelving for dishes and serving ware, but the area may also incorporate a small sink for prep work or a desk. In some cases it's complete with a full sink, dishwasher, trash compactor, and all the dish storage, making it a stand-alone washroom as seen on page 51.

Architect Bobby McAlpine advocates what he calls a "working pantry," which is outfitted with "microwaves, coffeepots, beverage preparations, and all the things I don't want to see and that don't have anything to do with cooking a meal and enjoying the company of guests while doing so."

It's common these days for people to want more connection between their kitchen and living-dining space, not less, so newly built pantries are often situated just off the kitchen rather than between the kitchen and the dining room, as they once were.

TOP LEFT When the shelves are well planned and smartly spaced, even a small pantry can hold a wealth of supplies.

BOTTOM LEFT Any closet can be fitted with shelves and converted to pantry storage. These sliding glass doors don't swing into traffic, and they hint that this is not a coat closet.

TOP RIGHT AND BOTTOM RIGHT A full wall of cabinetry that includes pantry cabinets or pullout trolleys can pack tremendous storage into far less space than a walk-in.

OPPOSITE PAGE The way to maximize storage is to use every vertical inch. In this pantry, even the space over the threshold is fitted with shelves.

Food Pantries

Food pantries are also gaining in popularity and can be created in various ways. Again, this is due at least in part to the shift in attitude against upper cabinets and toward an increasing desire for windows and openness. But most households need places to put canned goods and paper products. Some require both upper cabinets and extra pantry space—it all depends on the size of your family, the amount of cooking you do, and whether you prefer to buy in bulk.

A walk-in pantry is a luxury, but it needn't be big to have a big impact. A closet fitted with shelves—and perhaps some deep drawers or baskets—can hold as much as an entire bank of upper cabinets, with most of it easier to reach. If you don't have the space to create a new pantry, think about converting an existing broom closet. Traditional wall closets, with the characteristic pair of sliding doors, also make great pantries. And then there are cabinet-based solutions. A full-height pantry cabinet can be fitted with narrow bins and pullout shelves for extra efficiency. Or consider full-height pullout trolleys (shown above) lined up in a wall of cabinetry.

DESIGNER MICHELLE REIN ON

Organization

The key to successful storage of any kind is being organized, Michelle Rein points out. "A pantry isn't an area to just stuff in as much as you can. A bigger pantry can be a problem for some people." Try not to store more than you can see, and keep an eye on expiration dates when buying perishables in bulk.

Open and Closed Storage

A small shelving unit built to match the island ties this wall into the cabinetry and adds extra storage, both open and closed.

While taking stock of your belongings and weighing storage versus display, keep in mind both past and future acquisitions. "You don't want to store things you don't use, and now is the perfect opportunity to edit," says designer Kathy Farley. "Your kitchen should be designed so that the things you use the most are easily accessible."

Built-In Shelving

Whether you use it as part of the cabinetry or a separate unit, make room for some built-in shelving. Shelves add dimension to a space dominated by doors and drawer fronts, and they offer a place to display a collection, keep cookbooks within easy reach, and perhaps even house a television. A shelving unit may be divided for multiple purposes—shelves sharing space with slots or cubbies, some of which may take doors or drawers. In planning the configuration (as in all storage planning), be sure to allow room for the contents to grow—especially cookbooks, which have a way of multiplying.

TOP RIGHT This rustic wood-paneled kitchen has a white storage niche that complements the rest of the built-in cabinetry and offers a practical and eye-catching place for frequently used items.

BOTTOM RIGHT Sunk into the wall, this roomy unit combines drawers with shelving, some behind glass doors. The visible presence of dishes, cookbooks, baskets, and canisters brings life to the space.

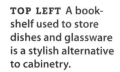

TOP LEFT A bookshelf used to store dishes and glassware is a stylish alternative to cabinetry.

MIDDLE LEFT A modified bookshelf sized to fit and tucked into the baseboard looks like a built-in and brings ample mixed storage to a formerly empty corner.

BOTTOM LEFT The island in this vintage-styled kitchen serves as a work surface with storage underneath. Open shelves nearby hold all the essentials for a creative baker.

Freestanding Furniture

Whatever the style of your kitchen, it can benefit from the inclusion of a piece of storage furniture, particularly since adding furniture is the surest way to inject some character into the space. China cabinets, armoires, bookshelves, and even worktables can be adapted for use in a kitchen as long as their shelves are sturdy enough to handle the weight of whatever you might put on them. An armoire dedicated to stacks of dishes or heavy pots, for example, might need to be retrofitted with properly spaced and reinforced shelves.

As an architect, Bobby McAlpine likes to incorporate freestanding storage in a kitchen because it can be updated more easily than cabinetry and doesn't threaten the architectural integrity of the space. "I'm primarily looking for ways to store things that aren't going to date the structure," he says, so he keeps built-ins minimal and timeless. He approaches cabinets "in a way that (future renovators) won't be inclined to revisit" and augments with freestanding pieces.

A large, sturdy armoire fitted with shelves makes a striking pantry. In the freestanding island, deep drawers, a shelf, and large baskets offer added storage.

This Shaker-style china cabinet was custom built and plumbed for a wet bar. It looks like a freestanding heirloom piece in which dinnerware and serving pieces have been kept for generations.

Open Shelves

The trick with open shelving is making sure that the shelves are sturdy enough for the job they're put to and that their contents are worthy of being stored in plain sight. Sturdiness is a factor of the thickness of the shelf, its means of support, and the intervals at which it's supported. There are numerous styles of shelf brackets to choose from for visibly supported shelves, and they can be an important design element. "Floating" shelves have supports that go from the wall directly into the core of the shelf, so they're invisible. Either floating or bracketed shelves can be reinforced by a cleat, a narrow strip of wood running along the wall under the rear edge of the shelf that prevents sagging. The longer or thinner the shelf, the more supports it needs, whether visible or concealed.

Open shelves demand neatness and collect dust, which means they're not for everyone. "Some people don't want to deal with keeping open storage clean," says Michelle Rein, "but it's beautiful if you can do it." The objects on display look best when they're grouped by type—stacks of plates together in one spot, glassware in another, for instance. Items that match or coordinate look even better, which makes collections prime candidates for open storage. One approach is to stick to a single color or a simple palette—all white objects with clear glassware is the most common. However, a display of colored objects on open shelves is a quick way to bring color into a space. Picture a collection of Fiestaware or Jadeite and you'll get the idea. And remember that swapping out what's on the shelves is an easy way to transform the look of your kitchen whenever you like.

OPPOSITE PAGE
This elegant all-white kitchen has a dining area with a recessed storage wall that features a built-in sideboard. Graceful open shelving displays a collection of iron-stone and glassware.

TOP RIGHT Shelves and their supports can take many forms. Displaying colorful objects and collections such as green glass means instant color for the room.

BOTTOM RIGHT Open shelving backed with bead-board paneling creates the feeling of a country kitchen. White dishes and repetitive clear canisters for dry goods offer simple storage.

Appliance Garages

A relatively new solution to an old problem, the appliance garage is a way to keep your countertop from getting cluttered with a toaster, blender, stand mixer, and coffeemaker. These are things you may use often enough that you don't want to have to haul them out of a cabinet every time—especially those that are unwieldy—but that you don't necessarily want to look at all day either. An appliance garage—which can take many forms, as shown here—will keep them at counter level but out of sight, thanks to a roll-up door or hideaway cubby.

TOP LEFT Ribbed glass makes a design element of these multiple garages. The lift-and-retract doors make it easy to get to the appliances.

BOTTOM LEFT This classic appliance garage with roll-up door has been stocked as a self-contained coffee station.

TOP RIGHT Small doors that match the rest of your cabinets will hide anything.

BOTTOM RIGHT This stand-mixer solution is a counter-height lift that lowers into the cabinet when not in use.

OPPOSITE PAGE Recessing a garage into a wall requires planning. Start thinking about it when laying out your kitchen storage.

Drawers and Pullouts

Michelle Rein has been designing and building custom cabinetry long enough that traditional undercounter cabinets seem to her a distant memory. "I have recollections of my parents' kitchen," she says, "where all the lower shelving is just behind cabinet doors and you have to bend over and fish around to find what you're looking for. Kitchens were horrible!" If you've ever parked yourself on the floor to find a pot lid in the far reaches of a cabinet, you understand Rein's sentiment. Thankfully, pullouts and deep drawers with full-extension glides have changed how kitchens function. "It's incredible that you can pull a drawer all the way out and see everything that's in it. It's night and day. Forget about fixed undercounter shelving," Rein says.

Stronger glides have enabled drawers to get bigger and to hold more weight, making them increasingly popular alternatives for dish and pot storage. But keep in mind the height of their contents. A too-deep drawer, for example, will waste valuable space. Pullouts—think of them as shelves on gliders—can be installed flush with the cabinet fronts, just like drawers, or be tucked behind doors. Like drawers, pullouts allow easy access to items stored all the way at the back. They can be spaced at close intervals to match their contents' height, and

ABOVE Full-extension drawers make heavy objects easy to access, while adjustable peg dividers keep contents tidy.

OPPOSITE PAGE, TOP LEFT What could be handier than pots in drawers right below the stove?

OPPOSITE PAGE, TOP RIGHT This drawer, with a deceptively tall front, disguises a pullout spice rack.

OPPOSITE PAGE, BOTTOM LEFT If you like to stow your pots rather than display them, open-front pullouts offer optimal access.

OPPOSITE PAGE, BOTTOM RIGHT A deep, divided drawer keeps cutting boards and cooling racks handy.

some are even adjustable like shelves. Most people still prefer under-counter storage to be enclosed—either in drawers or behind doors—because the lower shelves are located, the more dust and debris they collect. The advantage of a drawer over a pullout is that you don't have doors to deal with. But pullouts behind retractable doors offer the best of both worlds.

If you don't have the luxury of replacing your old fixed-shelf cabinets, you can still take advantage of sliding storage advances. Organizational stores and home improvement centers sell pullout trays of all shapes and kinds that can be attached to your fixed shelves or interior cabinet walls.

OPPOSITE PAGE, TOP LEFT Pullouts can be spaced according to their contents and tucked behind doors just like shelves. Retractable doors keep things clean but move out of the way when needed.

OPPOSITE PAGE, TOP RIGHT Pullout trolleys can be divided both vertically and horizontally, making all the contents easy to see and reach.

OPPOSITE PAGE, BOTTOM LEFT Another way to change up your fixed-shelf cabinets is to remove the doors and line the shelves with baskets, which can be easily transported to wherever the contents are needed.

OPPOSITE PAGE, BOTTOM RIGHT Sorting the recycling and compost becomes a quick and easy job when two receptacles can be hidden away side by side in a pull–out garbage bin.

RIGHT Fixed shelves can be augmented with a wide range of wire baskets on sliders and rails, found in retail stores.

Plate and Pot Racks

Because plates and pots are in constant use, storing them smartly is one of the primary considerations in kitchen functionality. In many cases, plates and pots are heavy, so stacks of them—whether in drawers, pullouts, or cabinets—can be difficult to manage. Racks make sense, as you can access any single plate or pot without having to wrestle it from a stack; having your plates and pots out in the open furthers that accessibility. If you are a plate collector or have a particularly beautiful set of pots, then so much the better—they'll dress up the space.

Plate racks come in many forms. A narrow rack with a brace across the front will hold plates facing forward, making a display of them (see page 118). Deeper racks with vertical dividers hold more plates in less space, so they're a more hardworking storage option but leave you looking at the edges of the plates rather than the fronts. Whatever form of plate storage you choose, there are at least two schools of thought about location. One maintains that plates should be stored as near as possible to the seating area, for easy table setting. The other maintains that they should be stored near the sink and dishwasher, making them easy to put away.

Pots are best stored near the stove, of course, which is why racks are generally hung over the stove or right next to it. A rack over an island is the kitchen equivalent of a chandelier over a dining table. The basis of a pot rack—hooks on a rod—is straightforward and can be adapted in any number of ways, from pots hung on coat racks to S-hooks on wall-mounted rods to large hanging grids with integrated hooks. As with any open storage, neatness is a factor. With pot racks in particular, so is size. A too-big rack or an abundance of pots can quickly overwhelm a space, so keep your pot rack proportional and organized.

Bear in mind, too, that anything used to support lots of plates or pots must be well anchored to the wall or ceiling to support the weight.

OPPOSITE PAGE For a compact kitchen where storage is at a premium, think vertically. A hanging pot rack suspended from the ceiling near the stove or sink makes access easy. Wall-mounted shelves and spice racks keep clutter off counters.

TOP RIGHT A simple iron bar hung with S-hooks is a time-honored way of storing pots and pans. In this kitchen, the pot rack is off to the side but framed by a window for added visual interest.

BOTTOM RIGHT This divided box sunk into the frame of an upper cabinet case provides an unexpected mix of colorful storage.

Wine Racks

Wine tasting is on the rise, which has more and more home-owners incorporating wine storage into their kitchens. The basic facts of wine storage are that wine is best kept in the dark and at a reasonably constant temperature, ideally a bit lower than room temperature. (Cold and heat are equally threatening.) If you're storing fine wines and intend to keep them for years, don't keep them in your kitchen, where temperatures fluctuate. But for younger inexpensive or mid-range wines and short-term storage, keeping wine in the kitchen, where it's easily accessed, will be fine as long as you carve out a space that's away from any heat sources (including the stove and dishwasher) and not in direct sunlight.

Wine is traditionally stored so as to keep the cork damp—a dried-out cork can lead to problems—so essentially all wine racks hold bottles either on their sides or inverted. The most popular approaches are individual cubbyholes and larger cubbies with X-braces for stacking bottles. For new wines that have plastic corks or metal screw caps, storing the bottles on their sides in individual cubbies still makes sense because it keeps the wine in the dark and makes each bottle accessible. But there's nothing wrong with standing bottles without natural corks in a dark, cool cabinet.

Spice Racks

Spice storage is always a challenge. Because spices don't keep forever, they come in small containers. But those small containers can waste a lot of shelf space, so they require smart storage that's scaled to fit. Spice racks can take the form of drawer inserts, narrow pullout trolleys, countertop displays, or shallow, closely spaced shelves. The best spice storage solutions are those that are positioned near the stove and allow you to see every label at a glance. Like wines, oils, and vinegars, spices are also best stored away from light and heat.

OPPOSITE PAGE Storing everyday wines in cubbyholes built into the cabinetry keeps them handy. It also makes the wine part of the kitchen landscape, just like pots on a rack.

ABOVE LEFT Shallow shelves built into the end of the island opposite the stove keep spices visible and easy to access.

ABOVE RIGHT The wall of this stove alcove was inset with a cabinet perfectly sized for spice bottles, keeping them at eye level and behind a closed door.

The Butler's Influence

THIS PAGE These kitchen cabinets were designed for maximum storage but also to reference the style of the original cabinetry in the adjacent butler's pantry (opposite).

OPPOSITE PAGE The butler's pantry is typical of its era, with a built-in hutch for linens and serving pieces opposite a service counter with an integral sink.

W hen the new owners of this early-20th-century home on a former naval base found the house, it had been empty for 10 years, stripped of all doorknobs and light fixtures. The Navy—no longer maintaining it as an officer's home—had long ago torn out the original kitchen cabinetry and replaced it with ill-fitting metal cabinets. But somehow the butler's pantry remained intact. Armed with a notebook of magazine photos and following the lead of the original pantry, the couple worked with general contractor and cabinetmaker Brian Eby to re-create what might once have been.

The Elements

- **Cabinets:** Painted custom frameless cabinets with combination of frame-and-panel and ribbed-glass fronts

- **Additional Storage:** Pantry closet and butler's pantry

- **Hardware:** Brass bin pulls, cut-glass knobs, and brass turn-locks

- **Counters:** White hex tile; butcher block beside stove; steel in butler's pantry

- **Backsplash:** White subway tile, with niche over stove

- **Sinks:** Single-basin ceramic main sink; integrated steel sink in butler's pantry

- **Appliances:** Refurbished antique stove; stainless-steel refrigerator; white dishwasher

- **Flooring:** Refinished Douglas fir subfloor

- **Finishing Touches:** Neutral palette; school-house lights; heirloom tea-towel cafe curtains

Q+A: Brian Eby talks about creating an efficient and authentic new kitchen in an abandoned naval officer's residence.

Being a cabinetmaker, when you saw the dingy metal cabinets in the kitchen of this stately old home, did you relish the chance to restore it to glory?

I was really excited, yes. I've never gotten to work on an ex-military base before. I loved the house and its scale, and it seemed like it'd be a fun kitchen to restore.

Was there ever any question about preserving the butler's pantry?

No, not really. I mentioned it at one point, thinking we could remove the doorway between it and the kitchen, which would give us a nice open floor plan. But the owners wanted to keep the two separate spaces, and they were very fond of the glass hutch. Plus, it was the only original work in that part of the house, so they were happy to see it stay.

And what about the little pantry off the main kitchen. What was that originally?

It was a closet that served the same function, but it didn't have any cabinetry —just some awkward shelves. It almost looked like cold storage. But the window in there was original, and we wanted to preserve it.

So, between the two pantries and the tall upper cabinets, this space pretty much has storage covered. And you've fitted the lower cabinets entirely with drawers.

I tend to steer people toward drawers because it's not always understood that with contemporary hardware you can have even heavy pots and pans in drawers, and we can adjust the drawer heights to get any configuration you need. You always come out ahead on usability, and there's not as much fatigue as when you're pulling things from the back of a cabinet. I think the drawers make it easier to keep things organized too, because you're lifting things out rather than constantly sliding things past one another. Lots of people want doors with pullouts behind them, but then you have to deal with the doors, and you also lose some width that way.

Is storage always the guiding principle for you when you're creating a kitchen from scratch?

It depends on the kitchen. If it's a home that's a showpiece for somebody who entertains and there's a service staff that deals with the reality of the cooking in a separate area, then it's sometimes "museum design," as I call it. For everybody else, yes, the storage and usability—that the space is comfortable to use—is the biggest issue. We can always make it look good once we've got the traffic flow and storage worked out, but it doesn't matter that it looks good if it doesn't work.

Do you get a lot of requests for tile counters these days?

I still get some requests. I'd say it's unusual but not unheard of. These clients were really specific about the aesthetic of tile as a nod to the history of the house. And they like tile—not all clients do. The price is coming down on some of the solid surface materials; it's no longer twice as much as tile, like it was at one time. So that has changed things.

The treatment behind the stove, with the little niche, was also the client's idea—from a picture in a magazine. Did you like the idea?

There's a brick chimney back there that's abandoned, and I initially wanted to expose it. But once I got over that, I thought this was a great way to add some space and depth to that area. The stove that they chose is so big that the cabinets alongside it got really narrow and it was feeling a little cramped. Adding that tile and recess—and the molding around the top—made it feel more intentional and ample. It didn't add much in terms of storage, but it pulled the space together.

What's your favorite thing about the finished kitchen?

The little pantry closet with the sliding door. When you open it, it's sort of a temple to efficiency. And with the window in there and the frosted glass door, there's a sort of prism effect. It makes the whole kitchen feel bigger, and it's just super-functional.

BELOW The homeowners knew right away they wanted an antique stove and found this one at the website of a nearby refurbisher.

RIGHT, TOP The owners debated about an existing awkward closet but decided to convert it to a food pantry behind a ribbed-glass pocket door with reproduction handle.

MIDDLE There are no fixed-shelf lower cabinets anywhere in this kitchen, Eby being an advocate of big drawers with full-extension glides.

BOTTOM The tile counter goes a long way toward making the new kitchen feel authentic. The new drawer pulls match the originals on the pantry's built-in.

THIS PAGE With three walls of cabinetry and closets, there's no need for a bulky cabinet-based island. On casters, this lithe island does mixed duty: as a prep surface, a breakfast table, and a laundry folding station.

OPPOSITE PAGE, LEFT The kitchen is open on one side to the central dining area and the living spaces beyond. The whole house opens generously to the outdoors.

OPPOSITE PAGE, RIGHT The laundry and broom closets are closed off by doors on sliding rails. To the left of the laundry closet, a mini-fridge beneath a cabinet of glassware forms a stand-alone beverage station.

Kathy Farley's moderately sized, three-sided kitchen combines a kitchen and laundry room into one. But by mixing in clerestory windows, open shelving, and cool colors, she's retained a sense of openness. (The leggy island also helps.) When your storage is as well planned as hers is, you needn't be shy about arranging coffee cups, cooking utensils, and market-fresh produce right out in the open.

The Elements

- **Cabinets:** Custom stained face-frame cases with combination of flat and grooved fronts; uppers in multiple depths

- **Island:** On steel legs and casters; top with overhang for seating

- **Additional Storage:** Floating corner shelves; laundry closet and broom closet with doors on sliding rails

- **Hardware:** Brushed stainless knobs and bar pulls

- **Counters:** White marble; butcher block between sink and stove; zinc on island

- **Backsplash:** White subway tile

- **Sink:** Stainless undermount single-basin with wall-mounted faucet and counter-mounted purified-water tap

- **Appliances:** Stainless-steel range, hood, microwave, refrigerator, dishwasher; white washer and dryer; wine fridge with paneled front

- **Flooring:** White oak with a custom gray-olive stain

- **Seating:** Mix-and-match counter stools; custom walnut table with matching benches

- **Finishing Touches:** Violet and robin's-egg blue palette with accents of white; picture window and clerestory windows; recessed lights; displayed dishware in white plus shades of blues and greens

Farley's kitchen is all about efficiency. Everything a cook needs is out in the open and close at hand: utensils on a rail to the left of the stove; oils and a timer on the shelf above it; knives in a slit in the butcher block; and serving pieces and glassware on open shelves.

"I really like to focus on layout in a kitchen. I give my clients a survey about how they live and how they use the kitchen—how many dishes, pots, and pans, how do they cook, how do they live, what do they think they're going to acquire—so that there's a place for everything. A kitchen should be designed so that the things you use all the time are accessible."
—Designer Kathy Farley

The Big Island

Keeping the dishes white, the furnishings and frames wood, the photos black and white, and the surfboard natural makes for a space that might otherwise feel kitschy.

L ots of warm wood, sunlight, and white beadboard provide the perfect backdrop for an understatedly nostalgic scene, where collections of white dishware and beach memorabilia are displayed with equal prominence. Though new, the glass-front cases seem as much like they could have come from a storefront of another era as does the big island at the heart of it all. A marble top on the island houses both sinks, allowing for a teak rear counter that matches the cabinetry.

The Elements

- **Cabinets:** Teak with paneled fronts

- **Additional Storage:** Stacked dishware cabinets with sliding glass fronts

- **Island:** Freestanding with large drawers and shelf

- **Hardware:** Wooden knobs

- **Counters:** Teak; white marble on island

- **Backsplash:** Integral to stove only

- **Sinks:** Twin white undermount sinks in island, one with restaurant-style sprayer

- **Appliances:** Stainless-steel refrigerator, dishwasher, and range with matching hood

- **Flooring:** Dark hardwood

- **Seating:** Midcentury Danish table and assorted chairs

- **Finishing Touches:** Wood and white color palette; beadboard; vintage surfboard, beach photos and maps, wire baskets, and ice cream parlor stools

An antique mercantile table, complete with deep drawers and a long shelf for storage, has been topped with white marble and fitted with a pair of sinks. The restaurant-style appliances and sprayer are as much a match for the space as the vintage stools. Mismatched midcentury chairs and a display of beach photos bring ample charm to the room.

Chapter 8

Finishing Touches

When decorating other rooms in your house, you'd focus on colors, furniture styles, fabrics, lamps, artwork, and all of the other elements that convey your style. Yet many people forget about those elements when it comes to the kitchen. It's the heart of the home, the hub of activity, and the place where family and friends inevitably gather, so why not treat it like any other living area?

A coat of slate gray paint, an antique cabinet, a cotton dhurrie rug, and a silver-framed painting are just some of the design choices that make this standard kitchen feel special.

A kitchen can be both beautiful and functional," says Michelle Rein. "Don't be afraid to make a statement of personality with it." There are myriad ways to personalize your space, though some kitchen elements are more easily updated than others, so let your long-term goals be your guide. Choose accent colors, lighting, window treatments, furniture, and accessories that are both appropriate to the house and in keeping with your style.

Color

It's simple to find ways to inject color into your kitchen. You will first want to decide how much color you want and how easy it will be to change the color should you tire of it. The conservative route is to keep the cabinets neutral, since it's a relatively big job to repaint them, and use color either on the walls or strictly in the accessories. Consider adding splashes of color with window treatments, banquette upholstery, or small countertop appliances. If that seems like too much of a commitment, display vibrant bowls or colored glassware on shelves—all of which can be easily swapped out by season or mood. If you want to go the bolder route by choosing a color for countertops or cabinets, take into account not only how long you can expect to like that color but, in the event you sell your house, how likely it is to appeal to buyers. And keep in mind that color calls attention to itself, which is why Kevin Price uses it to highlight his favorite features of a space.

The right colors for you will depend on the mood you want to create. Neutrals—from white and ivory (which are a suitable backdrop for any accent colors) through rich browns and even black—are a safe yet sophisticated choice. Sunny yellow is a timeless option for kitchens, while reds and oranges are a bolder choice. Certain shades of blue and green are classics in the kitchen—think of Jadeite green glassware or Delft blue china. But what's most important is that any color you choose be appealing for a space where you'll be working, relaxing, and enjoying food. In other words, this may not be the best place for a neon chartreuse or an ultraviolet purple.

OPPOSITE PAGE
A color palette of burnt orange walls and gray cabinets in this transitional kitchen was designed to complement the pairing of warm wood flooring and furnishings with cool stainless-steel appliances.

TOP RIGHT This blue and white kitchen offers a modern take on a traditional color scheme with one wall of cornflower blue glass subway tiles. Updated variations on woven seating and plaid window shades further modernize the classic cottage styling.

BOTTOM RIGHT The availability of laminate in the 1950s and '60s introduced the trend of using bright colors in the kitchen. Today, a shiny bank of cheerful yellow cabinets and shelving feels as retro as it does modern.

Walls and Ceilings

Although you want to treat your kitchen the same way you would any other room in the house, it's important to keep in mind that kitchen walls and ceilings must withstand both humidity and grease. Incorporating elements that are too delicate or difficult to clean isn't the best idea, which is why painted walls are more common than wall coverings, and semigloss and eggshell paints more common than flat. But don't rule out wallpaper altogether. While hand-painted and natural fiber papers can get ruined, smooth wallpapers are durable and easy to wipe clean. If your heart is set on a textured wall covering, such as grass cloth, look for a vinyl substitute or limit the material to an accent wall that's away from the range or sink.

A ceiling is often a missed opportunity for incorporating style. If the construction of your home allows, raising the ceiling height or adding a skylight can change a space significantly, and so can exposing beams and adding decorative treatments like crown molding or cove lighting. Consider painting the ceiling a paler hue of your wall color. If the surface is good and smooth, painting a ceiling a high-gloss white or iridescent neutral can reflect light and add shimmer to a candlelit dining area.

TOP LEFT In a room clad entirely in bleached knotty pine, the pitched-roof ceiling is a visual continuation of the walls, which makes the space feel larger and more open. Broken up with creamy white window trim, the overall effect is rustic and natural without being overbearing.

BOTTOM LEFT Don't underestimate the impact of one accent wall covered in boldly patterned wallpaper. Be sure to consider the practicality of wallpaper behind a range or sink, where it might be exposed to heat, steam, and grease.

OPPOSITE PAGE A full wall of chalkboard paint adds tremendous character to this neutral kitchen.

Windows

Several of our experts have noted that the most common request they hear from their clients is to increase the connection between the kitchen and the outdoors. Because the kitchen is often the household command post, it's important to be aware of what's happening outside, whether it's in the garden or the surrounding neighborhood, so the bigger the windows, the better.

Daylight is a tremendous asset to a kitchen, as is a striking view, and the style of windows is equally important. As with all other home elements, windows should be stylistically appropriate to the house. Contemporary spaces lend themselves to larger expanses of glass than older houses, in which groupings of windows with multiple panes are more suitable. For the ultimate kitchen window, there are many options in sliding glass doors that neatly break down the barrier between indoors and outdoors. Nothing is quite as convenient as direct access from a kitchen to an outdoor dining area or barbecue.

Regardless of style, you want windows that are energy efficient. Multipaned windows trap air—and sometimes argon gas—between the panes, providing a layer of insulation. The glass can also be tinted or coated to filter damaging ultraviolet rays and to deflect heat. And if you live in an urban area or on a busy street, look for sound-dampening options.

Then there's the matter of window coverings. Sunlight tends to trump any privacy concerns when it comes to kitchen windows, since kitchens often face the backyard and few of us cook in the buff. Also, glass is extremely easy to clean, while curtains are not. Consider forgoing coverings and concentrating instead on beautiful windows if you have privacy and a view. You may want to consider your choice of cabinet door styling when selecting new window frames. Sticking with the same simplicity or traditional craftsmanship will help keep the elements feeling integrated.

If you need light control or privacy, look for easy-to-launder cafe curtains or non-fabric options such as wood or bamboo blinds. If you live in a pleasant climate, make sure that the windows are easy to open and that they open wide. Nowhere is fresh air more welcome than in a kitchen.

ABOVE Maximize daylight by adding windows as tall as possible and extending them right down to counter level.

Lighting

Proper lighting is critical for a kitchen, where you need both clean, bright task lighting and warm, welcoming atmospheric lighting. Track lighting systems and rows of recessed lights are both popular choices because they can be positioned for task lighting while also providing ambient light for the space. But the look of pendant light fixtures—either one statement piece or a series of hanging lamps—can go a long way toward reinforcing the style of your kitchen. And don't rule out the beauty of a single accent lamp placed on an uncluttered portion of the countertop. Kathy Farley thinks lighting offers a perfect opportunity to impart personality because the range of available types, styles, and colors is so diverse.

Of course, having many options can also be daunting. Contemporary spaces often stick to the most minimal approach—recessed lights only—while period reproduction fixtures are wildly popular in renovated older homes. Traditional chandeliers are increasingly common in kitchens, particularly those that serve as both kitchen and dining area. Perhaps the biggest trend is the repetition of multiple fixtures— pendant lights hung in threes or twin schoolhouse lights over an island. Depending on the size of your space, you may want a mix of fixtures—for instance, recessed lights combined with a chandelier. Under-cabinet lighting is often the key to adding dimension and avoiding shadows in the primary prep areas. When combined with a single dimmable overhead fixture, this may be all that's needed to illuminate your kitchen.

TOP LEFT A pair of chrome schoolhouse-style pendant lamps offer task lighting in this kitchen. They also echo the retro look of the leather-and-chrome barstools.

BOTTOM This minimalist kitchen is filled with light, yet the fixtures are virtually invisible. Under-cabinet spots illuminate the cream backsplash, and a subtle fixture is suspended over the island.

OPPOSITE PAGE An ultra-modern kitchen makes the most of the various levels of this space. Under-cabinet fluorescent task lighting is combined with a trio of dim-mable halogen pendant lights over the breakfast bar.

TOP Two white chinoiserie barstools are not only convenient but help amp up the style quotient at this kitchen's peninsula breakfast bar.

BOTTOM A pair of bar-height benches offer guests a comfortable place to sit and watch a meal being prepared. They also allow flexible seating for up to four adults or six kids.

OPPOSITE PAGE, LEFT Colorful pillows and streamlined wicker chairs make this banquette breakfast nook inviting.

OPPOSITE PAGE, RIGHT This mix-and-match seating around a refectory table offers charm in an otherwise simple space. When combining different chairs, make them the same height.

Seating

The best kitchens are designed as much for function as they are for hospitality, which starts with offering guests a comfortable place to sit. But seating also presents a big chance to bring furniture into the mix.

Barstools pulled up to an island are beginning to replace the classic eat-in-kitchen area, as are wide, expansive spaces that merge the kitchen and dining room. In enclosed kitchens, space for a full-size dining table and chairs can be hard to come by, calling for extra creativity. That's why factoring in seating space is a critical part of the layout process. Give plenty of consideration to the kind of space you're creating and the kind of seating you prefer. Do you need to move chairs around, or could you build a dining nook? Are you more likely to sit down for breakfast at a small table or a taller counter? How many people do you need to accommodate? Don't overlook the possibility of building a bump-out—an addition small enough that no change is needed to the house's foundation or roofline. A bump-out may buy you just enough space for a small booth or a full-size dining table, depending on the specifics of your kitchen.

When it comes to choosing a style of stools or a table and chairs, take the same approach as in the rest of the house. For a sleek and contemporary look, consider streamlined furnishings and keeping chairs within a single silhouette. For an eclectic mix of new and vintage pieces, try mixing modern chairs with an old farmhouse table. Be aware that in most cases, people see the chairs, not the table, so they'll provide more of the style element. In any setting, a banquette—a bench built against a wall, with a table pushed up to it—is a great space-saving solution with nostalgic appeal. And in all choices, think ahead to cleaning and upkeep. Smooth table surfaces will keep cleanup simple, but don't think you have to forgo upholstery on benches, stools, and chairs. Just be careful about your choice of materials. Leather upholstered seats may offer the perfect patina when paired with an old wooden table, but food stains are hard to avoid. Martha Angus recommends outdoor fabrics, which are extremely durable and stain resistant.

Kathy Farley is thinking beyond a table and chairs for her next project. "I want sofas," she says. "People congregate in the kitchen, and I want them to be comfortable."

Decorative Accents

It can't be said too often that a kitchen is a room in which you spend a great deal of time and that it should offer the same pleasures and comforts of any other room. There's no reason you can't include accents like artwork, rugs, and accessories—you just have to be thoughtful in choosing them.

As noted, cooking and cleaning up generate humidity and grease, both of which can take their toll on natural fibers and delicate possessions. In choosing collectibles to display on cabinet tops or open shelves, stick to things that can be periodically wiped clean. The same goes for selecting artwork, especially if it will be hung near the stove or dishwasher. An oil painting on canvas—which can take a wiping from a damp sponge once or twice a year—is a reasonably safe choice as long as it's not too close to the stove, as are artworks framed behind glass. Glass is easy to clean, but humidity can still warp the paper, so keep an eye on framed pieces.

Rugs are a welcome addition to hard kitchen floors, especially near the sink and stove. But any rug will receive a great deal of foot traffic as well as inevitably have food dropped on it. Rugs should be durable, non-slip, and machine washable, so keep your selections to woven and braided cotton varieties or the newer options in woven recycled plastic. If your family is a relatively tidy bunch and you want the drama of a fancier rug, it's wise to stick to patterns that will hide stains.

Larger decorative accents might be structural or architectural. For instance, you might consider a built-in cabinet fashioned to look like an antique hutch, a porthole window that reinforces a beach theme, or a decorative tile treatment to bring color, pattern, and personality into the room in a single gesture. Ultimately, every part of your kitchen—from the cabinets and countertops to the plate racks and dinnerware—is a design element. Striking a balance between style and function will help keep your kitchen from feeling cluttered while making it your favorite room in the house.

DESIGNER
ERIK BARR ON

Artwork in Kitchens

Erik Barr features art throughout his condo, including a painting next to his range (see page 142). For that spot he chose a piece that can be wiped off from time to time, and he stays mindful of its presence. As he puts it, "You just don't point the teakettle in that direction."

OPPOSITE PAGE, TOP Nothing personalizes a kitchen like a treasured collection. This one also brings color to the mix.

OPPOSITE PAGE, BOTTOM The most utilitarian objects can create a beautiful display when pared down and arranged in groupings. Consider open shelves for storing your well-worn wooden cutting boards or a trio of ironstone water pitchers.

RIGHT A display of artwork and graphic decorative letters turns this all-white kitchen into a gallery of style. Pops of red and other bright colors combined with wood and woven baskets on open shelving create a mod, cheerful vibe.

Case Study

Indoor-Outdoor Kitchen

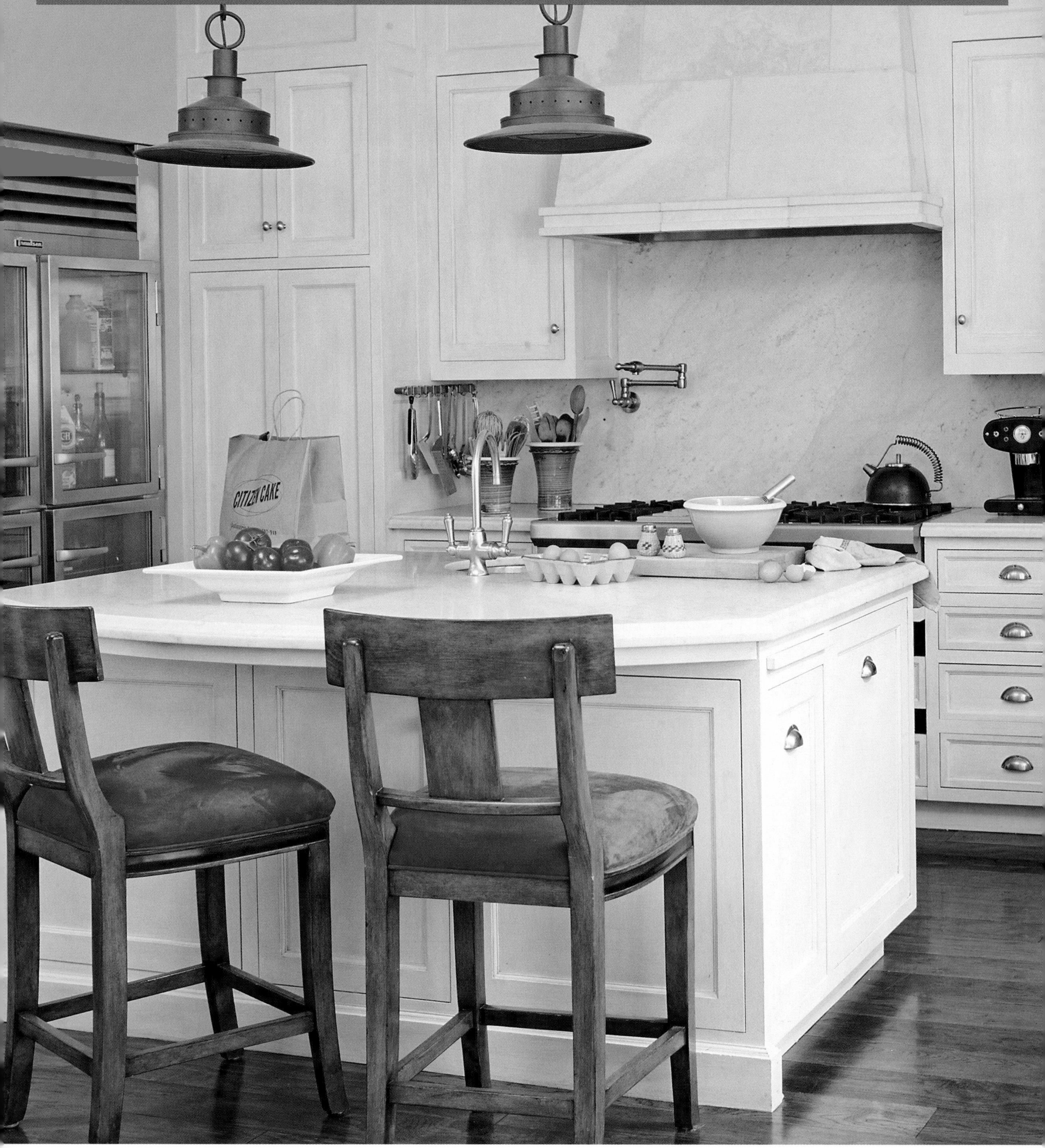

Marble counters and glazed cabinetry provide a neutral backdrop for brightly upholstered barstools, marine-style pendant lights, and a glass-front fridge.

Asked to create a combination family room and kitchen for a San Francisco family with a son, designer Martha Angus knew it would need to be a "very sturdy" space, especially since it opens onto a garden via French doors. A family room demands comfy, upholstered furnishings, so she relied heavily on durable outdoor fabrics. But she still pulled together a refined space well suited to the rest of the home.

The Elements

- **Cabinets:** Face-frame cases with flush-mounted doors and drawers, molding detail

- **Island:** Of matching cabinetry; top with overhang for seating

- **Hardware:** Brushed nickel knobs and bin pulls

- **Counters:** White Carrara marble

- **Backsplash:** Matching marble slab

- **Sinks:** Multi-basin stainless-steel undermount main sink; matching prep sink in island

- **Appliances:** Commercial glass-door refrigerator; double wall ovens in black; stainless-steel gas cooktop with built-in hood

- **Flooring:** Wide-plank hardwood

- **Seating:** Built-in upholstered booth with nailhead detail; French lava-stone pedestal table; upholstered barstools; loveseat and armchairs upholstered in outdoor fabrics

- **Finishing Touches:** Red, khaki, and sage palette; French doors; tilt-out windows; iron pendant lights; matchstick blinds; wall-mounted television, recessed and framed

Q+A: Designer Martha Angus talks about creating an elegant space that can also withstand a young family.

You kept the structural parts of this kitchen classic, elegant, and entirely neutral. And then you brought in lots of color in other ways. Is that an approach you often take?
Yes, that's definitely how I like to do things: Keep it clean and classic, and then pull in color with artwork and upholstery. I hate to do anything that isn't going to age well, and when you have an older home, it's important to do what's correct for the home. So I like a neutral base.

The space is equal parts kitchen and family room. How did you weight those differing demands against each other? And how did you manage to strike such a good balance between the formal and the casual?
The husband is in finance, and I knew he wanted to be able to see business news, even when cooking. So we've got the TV there, recessed into a niche above the fireplace, with a nice-looking frame around it. The family also has cats, so we wanted to do something animal-proof. And the door to the courtyard is right there, which means debris comes in, so it needed to be a very sturdy kitchen.

The little built-in dining booth is enchanting, and the table quite helpfully has no feet. What's the tabletop made of?
It's a pedestal table, which is important in a tight space like that, so you can scoot around it easily. And the top is fabulous: It's French lava stone. The wife, who is a friend of mine, picked it out, and it's the exact color of her eyes. She spends summers in the south

of France and wanted some French touches, so we had the leather upholstery stained and stamped with a damask pattern. It's not a very big kitchen, and we were trying to maximize the space, so that's what led to the built-in.

A lot of people shy away from using fabrics in a kitchen, thinking they'll be too hard to keep clean. But this kitchen is a great example of how much impact some upholstery can have.
Exactly. I love using lots and lots of outdoor fabric in kitchens because it's so durable, and it's no longer just stiff sailcloth. It feels like any other fabric, so why not use it?

The pendant lights are another element that adds a lot to the character of the space. What's the story on those?
We found them in L.A., and the client and I both just loved them.

And the finish on the cabinets isn't quite as simple as it first appears. Can you tell us about their paint job?
They're glazed. My trick with any cabinets, kitchen or bathroom, is to paint them in a 50-50 mix of Benjamin Moore's Linen White and Decorator White. So that's what we did here, and then an artist came in and added a glaze to make them look soft and more antique.

How did you settle on the glass-door refrigerator for this space? And is it actually a commercial fridge?
It is commercial, and we didn't bargain on the compressor, which makes a huge amount of noise. So we put it in the next room. The owner is very into cooking and is really neat and tidy, but she's told me that with the glass doors you have to be immaculate. But she still loves the fridge.

OPPOSITE PAGE, TOP A loveseat and armchairs covered in outdoor fabrics make for worry-free comfort.

THIS PAGE AND BOTTOM LEFT In the charming yet sensible booth, the pedestal table has no feet to clog up the space, and the stamped leather upholstery wipes clean. Matchstick blinds filter the sunlight.

Sitting Pretty

THIS PAGE For this refined kitchen, the owners chose an antique table and chairs rather than an island.

OPPOSITE, CLOCKWISE FROM TOP In addition to the oversized floral print, the walls are lined with amusing dog portraits in gilt frames.

The colors are kept to soft yellow and apricot. A patch of yellow tile on the diagonal adds subtle interest over the stove.

A collection of blue-and-white pottery behind glass doors adds another dimension to the space and palette.

This Boston kitchen has all the elegance of a traditional sitting room, but with a dash of humor. The walls and windows are treated to a large-scale floral print, the furniture is antique, the counters are classic New England soapstone, and the architectural detailing is generous. But the walls are lined with beautifully framed dog portraits. Those, the striped chair cushions, and the casual diamond-patterned rug keep the space from tipping into fussiness.

The Elements

- **Cabinets:** Painted face-frame cases with flush-mounted fronts and crown molding detail; glass-front uppers

- **Hardware:** Polished nickel bin pulls and turn-locks

- **Counters:** Soapstone

- **Backsplash:** Glazed ceramic squares, laid in bordered diamond pattern behind stove

- **Sink:** Stainless-steel undermount single basin with exposed-bridge faucet

- **Appliances:** Stainless-steel refrigerator, wine cooler, dishwasher, and wall oven; ceramic smooth-top cooktop; built-in hood

- **Flooring:** Oak

- **Seating:** Antique table and chairs

- **Finishing Touches:** Yellow and apricot palette; floral wall treatment with matching Roman shades and coordinating-stripe seat cushions; billiards-style light fixture; checked rug; dog portraits; blue-and-white dishware behind glass doors

THIS PAGE A classic red Aga stove sets a cheerful tone in this casual kitchen.

OPPOSITE PAGE, TOP Open shelving, cup hooks, and a pot rack keep everything as handy as can be. The colorful dishware enlivens the room.

OPPOSITE PAGE, BOTTOM The modest table and wicker chairs continue the casual tone. A wall-mounted television is positioned where everyone can see it.

For the ultimate in a happy and casual live-in kitchen, this designer-homeowner combined a red Aga stove with white beadboard, butcher block, red wicker, and Roman shades in a lively print. To brighten things up even more, she displayed a collection of dishware in an array of colors on open shelving supported by decorative brackets. A restaurant-size refrigerator, built-in desk, and wall-mounted television round out the welcoming offerings.

The Elements

- **Cabinets:** Painted face-frame base cabinets with flush-mounted fronts, no toe-kick

- **Island:** Of matching cabinetry

- **Additional Storage:** Open shelving; chrome pot rack; built-in desk

- **Hardware:** Polished nickel bin pulls and knobs

- **Counters:** Solid surface; butcher block on island

- **Backsplash:** Solid-surface curb; subway tile over range

- **Sink:** White apron front

- **Appliances:** Red Aga stove; stainless-steel dishwasher and commercial fridge

- **Flooring:** Stone tile in mix of squares and rectangles

- **Seating:** Simple pine table with red wicker chairs; chrome barstools

- **Finishing Touches:** Red-and-white patterned Roman shades; beadboard with molding trim; shelf brackets; recessed lights; whitewashed exposed beams; collection of brightly colored dishware

A Chance of Sand

THIS PAGE The industrial pendant lights look as if they could have come from the owner's childhood retreat. The lamp on the kitchen counter is a quintessentially Southern touch.

OPPOSITE PAGE Open shelving holds everything from cookbooks and teacups to oyster plates and souvenirs.

The owner of this weekend home on the Florida coast wanted to re-create the relaxed cottage character of the fishing retreat that she remembers from her childhood. To do so, ceilings were lowered, walls paneled, and everything whitewashed for a fresh-scrubbed, nautical feeling. Durable surfaces stand up to sand and grime. Ticking-stripe shades and rag rugs reinforce the casual mood and are easily laundered.

The Elements

- **Cabinets:** Frameless base cabinets with grooved fronts

- **Island:** Of matching cabinetry

- **Hardware:** Blackened bronze wire pulls

- **Counters:** Polished granite

- **Sinks:** Undermount single-basin main and prep sinks with gooseneck faucets; pot filler

- **Appliances:** Stainless-steel professional-grade range, matching hood

- **Flooring:** Ebonized hardwood

- **Seating:** Stone-topped wood table with steel chairs

- **Finishing Touches:** Ticking-stripe Roman shades; white paneling and beams; industrial pendant lights; glass bottle lamp; oyster plates as wall art

Chapter 9

Getting It Done

After reading the previous chapters, you should have a better idea of the many considerations that come into play in planning a new kitchen, whatever its size and scope. Once you finish the questionnaire on pages 28 and 29 and assess the photos you flagged—along with your notes on why you flagged them—it's time to shift from dreaming mode into planning mode. It's time to make it all happen.

Even the smallest kitchen can be organized for efficiency. This one includes open storage for dishes, pots, and wine bottles, as well as both counter and table seating areas.

From Dreams to Reality

Collecting inspirational photos and looking for the consistencies among them will help you develop your initial dream kitchen. Photos and your notes can also help you keep the entire project on track, providing both budgetary and design guidance. "It's important for people to get everything out on paper so they understand the magnitude of what they want," says Erik Barr. "Often it's more than they can afford, so it's smart to go through it all and prioritize."

Prioritizing

It's a cold reality, but most people don't have the budget to do everything they want. However, before you begin striking things from your wish list, do some cost comparisons, get professional input, and try to let go of preconceptions about styles, materials, and brand names. After careful consideration, you might decide that the things you value most are not the ones you initially thought.

What advice do our experts have to offer when it comes to setting priorities? Brian Eby believes that "adequate storage and a functional layout are more important than aesthetic matters." Kathryn Rogers concurs: "A kitchen is about quality of life. You have to have places to put things." For Benjamin Nutter, it's a matter of longevity: "A kitchen is the working space of a home and where people spend their time, so we think about its use over time. It's the place in the house with the most moving parts, and it needs to stand up." Nutter strives to get the most functionality he can within a client's budget. Echoing that, Kathy Farley says, "Colors can always be painted out, but with materials I really want them to make sense for a long period of time."

"Spend money on the things you will touch every day," Barr says. "For instance, if you like to cook it might be worth it to you to have a nice stove. Cabinet hardware is a thing you touch every day, so that might be a priority. Or it might be the countertop and the sink." Cleanup is a constant in a kitchen, and Barr notes that the way a sink is set within a counter matters and is worth getting right.

While our panelists agree that a good stove is a wise investment for serious cooks, several feel that it's easy to overspend on appliances. "People tend to put in more appliances—and bigger appliances— than they need, which takes away storage space," says Michelle Rein. "So do you really need these things? Are you really going to use them?" Despite being an avid cook, Kathy Farley feels that an eight-burner range rarely makes sense—"You'll never use eight burners at once"—and she notes that not all expensive appliances live up to their price tags. Farley, Rein, and Nutter all counsel clients to visit manufacturers' showrooms in their area and even to sign up for the cooking demonstrations that take place right in the showroom, allowing people to try out different appliances. "Be a savvy shopper," Rein says. "There are excellent appliances for less money that will give you a beautiful look for most kitchens. You don't have to spend top dollar."

Barr has one more piece of advice, which is to beware of the thing you covet most: "Often the thing you're digging in your heels about is the thing that has to go." He has experienced this situation not only with clients but with his own renovation. Letting go of the idea he was clinging to—preserving an original butler's pantry—changed the entire project for the better. "Having wiggle room is paramount," Barr says. "The ability to think outside the box is why you should bring in a professional in the first place, and what gives a professional a leg up. So don't get too attached to any one element."

A mix of high-end and affordable materials in this kitchen reveals a remodel that prioritized impactful design elements like the live-edge island top, the vibrant wall color, and the rich wood floor, all of which amp up the simple laminate cabinets and counters.

Enlisting Help

The type of professionals you'll need to work with to create your new kitchen depends on the scope of the project. If you're doing strictly cosmetic work, you may only need to hire someone to sand and paint your cabinets. Relocating receptacles, fixtures, sinks, and appliances requires the help of electricians

and plumbers. Other changes might call for carpentry, drywall, flooring or tile contractors. The more complicated the job—and the more numerous the contractors—the more important it is to have a general contractor to coordinate the work and oversee its quality as well as anticipate and apply for needed permits. Working with an architect or

interior designer can pay dividends, but be sure to choose one with extensive kitchen experience.

"If you're spending a good chunk of money to substantially improve your kitchen," says Brian Eby, "allocate 10 or 20 percent to hiring a professional designer or architect. They'll be able to help you get the most bang for your buck

LEFT The help of a designer or an architect can be extra important in a small space, where maximizing storage, bringing in light, marrying adjacent spaces, and getting every last detail right are paramount.

RIGHT With a back door that opens into the kitchen, the owners of this space wanted to include a mudroom in the renovation. The designers worked out a way for them to have one without sacrificing space or openness—they carved it into a half-wall separating the kitchen and family room.

and will also have a good handle on the resale considerations." As a general contractor, Eby has seen firsthand, time and again, the impact of professional clarity and objectivity: On your own, "you will do things the way you've had them before or have seen them done; a pro will have a different, unfettered perspective." Professionals also bring to the table ample knowledge of materials and appliances—and the pricing and availability thereof—potentially saving you both money and time.

When you are looking for a designer or general contractor, it's vital to interview multiple candidates and ask for references. Eby recommends contacting several references, visiting completed job sites—especially those with similarities to your project—and, of course, asking about performance with regard to budget and deadlines. "Anyone should be completely comfortable giving you those references—you're not being unreasonable in asking for them. And if anyone is hesitant about giving them to you, consider that a red flag." A good general contractor will have a regular roster of subcontractors, from painters to electricians, whom he or she has worked directly with in the past and can vouch for.

If you need design help but can't afford a trained architect or designer—and don't assume that without

interviewing a few—there are software programs available that will help you develop a floor plan. You'll also find "kitchen designers" on staff wherever cabinets are sold. These are employees trained in the use of computer modeling programs for translating a floor plan into 3-D, but they generally are not formally trained architects or interior designers. "They might not actually be good at thinking spatially," cautions Neal Schwartz. "Plus, their job is to sell cabinets, so they'll want to solve every problem with a piece of cabinetry when there may be a better option. You can wind up with inefficient cabinetry and a kitchen that doesn't take advantage of assets like the light or the flow of the space." So even with in-store pros, ask for and follow up on references to ensure you're working with someone who will improve on what you could do yourself.

Budgets and Schedules

"You'd think it would be obvious, but scheduling seems to be a challenge because we're all so used to getting things instantly," says Benjamin Nutter. "So we talk to clients quite a bit about schedule." Construction projects are disruptive and take time —notoriously longer than the estimate—so be prepared for the reality of having your kitchen out of commission for anywhere from one to 10 weeks for a custom remodel. Nutter raises the related issue of your availability once work begins. If you're able to meet regularly to discuss ideas, a project can be more flexible, with design decisions made as construction progresses. If your schedule prohibits that, you'll want the design to be more or less complete before the work begins.

ABOVE Custom cabinetry like this bank of storage may take more time and cost more money than stock cabinets, but the end result is a kitchen that feels permanent and unique and is often perfectly measured for your storage needs.

OPPOSITE PAGE Salvaged plank flooring and a number of freestanding elements —the island, wine rack, and bookshelf— are a large part of this kitchen's charm. Building a largely unfitted kitchen like this one also requires less construction and allows pieces to be added over time.

Then there's the extreme variability of costs beyond the general construction estimate. "Unlike the rest of the house," Nutter explains, "construction costs (for kitchens) can be misleading because they can easily double once you factor in cabinetry, counters, and appliances." Construction costs aren't nearly as flexible as your material costs will be. For example, the labor cost for laying a tile floor will depend almost strictly on square footage, so it will be largely the same regardless of the tile you choose. But the cost of the tile itself will vary drastically depending on whether it's linoleum or limestone. Drawing up a basic plan and getting labor bids early in the process will help you estimate the budget for materials. You may find you're more flexible about some aspect of the construction than you are about materials. For example, you may choose to forgo installation of a skylight in order to get that limestone floor.

On the subject of construction costs, Erik Barr notes, "Small jobs don't necessarily cost less. There's no economy of scale, and no contractor wants a small job anyway." In his experience, it doesn't make design or economic sense to constrain a contractor by clinging, for instance, to the position of a window or door. "People have this notion that if they keep it contained it'll keep the price down," he says, but it's not necessarily the case. Kathryn Rogers likes to show clients alternatives to what they think they want, along with comparative costs, because often the difference in the cost of a more substantive change is less than expected, and the results much greater. So she draws each project up three different ways and prices them out, and clients are consistently surprised.

Because remodeling projects are inherently unpredictable, every job has the potential to take longer and cost more than initially expected. If you can't afford to go over budget, don't price the job out at your full budget—set aside 15 to 20 percent for contingencies. For example, if you have $45,000 to spend and not a penny more, proceed as though you have only $35,000 and bid out all labor and materials to fall under that figure. Then you'll have some wiggle room to change your mind, and you'll be covered if it turns out your subfloor is rotten or the range you love gets discontinued and the new model costs more. For a major overhaul, ask your contractor for a job schedule, know the delivery windows on every material, fixture, and appliance, and make sure orders are placed such that elements are on hand as they're needed. Delays cost money.

Demolition and Deconstruction

Demolition on even the smallest scale raises environmental, safety, and health concerns ranging from hazardous construction materials to overtaxed landfills. In order to avoid the toxic fumes or particles—not to mention the inconvenience of an off-limits kitchen—you may consider decamping to a relative's home or nearby rental during demolition, sanding, or painting.

The primary hazard of demolition is that there's no telling what is in or under the floors, walls, ceiling, and even counter-top surfaces without cutting or tearing into them. But doing so in a home built before the 1980s can inadvertently unleash toxic and cancer-causing substances such as lead and asbestos. Most people associate lead with paint and asbestos with insulation, but there are numerous adhesives and construction materials—including floor and ceiling tiles and even fabrics—with asbestos content. There are also ceramic glazes that contain lead. (Imported tiles available today may still have lead content in their glazes.) Asbestos is hazardous only when airborne, so if an old floor is glued down and stable, your best bet is to leave it and put the new floor over it, in case the old flooring or the glue contains asbestos. If you plan to remove old flooring or wallpaper, sand painted surfaces, chisel out tile,

or cut into walls, test the surfaces before the work begins. Look for an accredited testing lab in your town, which should also be able to inform you about removal and disposal guidelines and requirements, should materials in your home test positive for hazardous substances.

Then there's the matter of waste. Anytime you can reuse existing materials or other elements in your kitchen—whether by refinishing existing cabinets or floors or refurbishing a stove—you will limit both the amount of waste you create and your consumption of newly manufactured materials, and you will likely save money in the process. When tearing out anything you won't reuse, strive to deconstruct rather than demolish. You can donate cabinets, sinks, and floorboards to various agencies or sell them to salvage companies, keeping the materials in circulation and, again, out of landfills. Your city may even require that you do so. Many municipalities now grant building permits contingent on waste-management plans, some mandating that a high percentage of removed materials be recycled or made available to salvage companies rather than sent to the landfill. All of this is good for you as well as for the planet, and the same salvage companies may have the reclaimed wood flooring you've been dreaming of.

Resources

The following are organizations, manufacturers, and retailers mentioned in this book, along with a variety of others you might find helpful in creating your new kitchen—with an emphasis on companies dedicated to environmentally responsible manufacturing processes and/or products.

Organizations

Energy Star
energystar.gov
The website of the joint program of the Environmental Protection Agency and the Department of Energy offers information and guidance on product selection and home improvements for energy savings.

Forest Stewardship Council
us.fsc.org
A multinational organization setting guidelines for sustainable forest management and offering guidance to consumers by way of their certification program.

National Kitchen & Bath Association
nkba.org
The website of this professional association for the kitchen and bath design industry offers tools and resources for homeowners, including a database of certified professionals, a gallery of inspirational images, and a virtual kitchen-planning tool.

WaterSense
epa.gov/watersense
This partnership program with the Environmental Protection Agency identifies and labels high-efficiency fixtures, including faucets, showerheads, toilets, and irrigation systems.

Manufacturers and Retailers

Adagio
modernreality.com/adagiosinks
Focused primarily on handcrafted sinks—including farmhouse sinks made of wood or carved of natural stone—Adagio also sells some countertop materials.

Aga
aga-ranges.com
Known for its classic enameled cast-iron ranges, the British company is now offering hoods, dishwashers, and full-size and undercounter refrigerators to match. Aga also has a stainless-steel line of goods.

Alkemi
alkemi.com
Creators of a solid-surface material that is a composite of at least 60% recycled aluminum scrap and polymeric resin. The material comes in several colors and can be cut and shaped with standard woodworking tools.

AlterEco
bamboocabinets.com
Makers of custom bamboo cabinetry (exclusive to the San Francisco Bay Area).

Ann Sacks
annsacks.com
An importer and manufacturer of stone, ceramic, and designer tiles, Ann Sacks is now a division of Kohler and offers sinks in stone and copper as well as a line of faucets.

Armstrong
armstrong.com
Best known for its flooring products—which include hardwoods, laminates, ceramic tile, vinyl, and linoleum—Armstrong also offers a range of ceiling products and a line of stock cabinets.

Bedrock Industries
bedrockindustries.com
Purveyors of tile handmade from 100% recycled glass. All packing and shipping materials are also recycled.

Benjamin Moore
benjaminmoore.com
Long favored by designers for its high-quality pigments, the paint company now also offers Eco Spec, a line of low-odor, low-VOC paints.

Berkeley Mills
berkeleymills.com
The FSC-certified furniture makers also craft custom kitchens from a variety of responsibly harvested woods.

Big Chill
bigchillfridge.com
Creators of refrigerators, dishwashers and stoves that meld Energy Star-approved efficiency with colorful 1950s styling.

Black's Farmwood
blacksfarmwood.com
A company that takes over old barns scheduled for demolition, salvages the siding and beams, and repurposes them for paneling, flooring, and a variety of other applications.

Brick Floor Tile Inc.
brick-floor-tile.com
Makers of clay brick tiles, available in two thicknesses and a range of colors.

Carlisle Wide Plank Floors
wideplankflooring.com
Makers of historical-style wood flooring in a variety of hardwoods and reclaimed woods.

Concreteworks
concreteworks.com
Using a lightweight cement-based composite, the company crafts countertops, tabletops, sinks, and more.

Corian
corian.com
Perhaps the best-known solid-surface material, distributed by DuPont.

Crossville Inc.
crossvilleinc.com
Tile manufacturer specializing in stone-look porcelain in a range of colors, sizes, and finishes.

EcoTimber
ecotimber.com
Specializing in FSC-certified hardwood and bamboo flooring, including engineered wood products and bamboo.

Eleek
eleek.com
Designer-manufacturers of hardware, sinks, and lighting, with an emphasis on handcrafting and a commitment to recycled products and sustainable practices.

EnviroGlas

enviroglasproducts.com
Suitable for both floors and countertops, Enviro-Glas suspends bits of tumbled recycled glass in epoxy resin for a terrazo-like surface.

Expanko

expanko.com
Offering a range of cork products, primarily flooring, as well as recycled rubber and combination cork and rubber flooring.

Fireclay Tile

fireclaytile.com
Makers of recycled and handmade tile with lead-free glazes as well as innovative new products, including Vulcanite, which is made from quarried volcanic lava, and glazed thin brick.

Formica

formica.com
Best known for its laminate products, the company manufactures a variety of surfaces, including metal, stone, and veneer, as well as sinks.

Globus Cork

corkfloor.com
Purveyors of cork tiles and floating floors with an emphasis on their wide range of vibrant colors.

Granada Tiles

granadatiles.com
Making traditional tile in Nicaragua with zero-waste manufacturing methods and lead-free pigments.

Green Depot

greendepot.com
National distributor of eco-friendly building supplies and household products.

Greenhome Solutions

ghsproducts.com
Family-run Seattle retailer offering a broad range of green building supplies online, including flooring, cabinetry, fixtures, tiles, and sealants.

Heath Ceramics

heathceramics.com
The legendary midcentury pottery company, under new management, is still manufacturing tiles and tableware in the company's aesthetic tradition and under stringent self-imposed recycling and reuse programs.

Continued

Henrybuilt
henrybuilt.com
Built-to-order cabinet systems organized into mix-and-match components and employing FSC-certified core and veneer wood products as well as recycled plastic and paper countertop materials.

The Home Depot
www.homedepot.com

IceStone
icestoneusa.com
Makers of recycled glass countertop and surfacing material manufactured in a zero-waste facility in Brooklyn, New York.

John Boos
johnboos.com
Since 1887, manufacturers of traditional butcher blocks as well as countertops, tabletops, cutting boards, and more.

Just Sinks
justsinks.com
Manufacturers of a wide range of stainless-steel sinks, faucets, and sink tops.

Kohler
kohler.com
A recognized leader in sinks and faucets.

KraftMaid Cabinetry
kraftmaid.com
Offering the widest selection of styles of built-to-order cabinetry.

La Cornue
la-cornue.net
Designed in 1908 and immortalized 100 years later in the movie Ratatouille, the enameled cast iron French range is a true kitchen icon. Now available in several styles and colors.

Lowe's
www.lowes.com

Marmoleum
forbo-flooring.com
The largest distributor of linoleum, in a variety of formats.

Natural Cork & More
naturalcork.com
A leader in cork flooring, the company also offers bamboo and hardwoods.

Neil Kelly Cabinets
neilkellycabinets.com
Cabinets built from sustainable materials, made with environmentally responsible techniques.

The Old Fashioned Milk Paint Co.
milkpaint.com
Makers of chemically safe, historically authentic paint, available in 20 colors.

PaperStone
paperstoneproducts.com
The only solid-surface material certified by the FSC, PaperStone suspends cellulose fiber in non-petroleum resin.

Plyboo
plyboo.com
Makers of formaldehyde-free bamboo plywood used as flooring, paneling, counters, tabletops, and cabinetry.

Rejuvenation
rejuvenation.com
Manufacturers of period reproduction light fixtures, hardware, and house parts, the company also deals in architectural salvage.

Restoration Timber
restorationtimber.com
Purveyor of richly grained old-growth hardwood reclaimed from barns, factories, and other structures built from trees that were cut down 100 years ago or more.

Richlite
richlite.com
Manufacturers of a paper and resin surface used for countertops and cutting boards.

Rocky Mountain Hardware
rockymountainhardware.com
Designers and manufacturers of rustic and modern hardware, sinks, and fittings hand cast of solid bronze containing at least 90% post-consumer recycled content.

Sonoma Cast Stone
sonomastone.com
Makers of handcrafted concrete countertops, sinks, tiles, and furniture.

Sunbrella
sunbrella.com
The leading manufacturer of outdoor fabrics, increasingly being used in kitchens and other indoor applications.

Teragren
teragren.com
Makers of fine bamboo flooring, panels, and veneer.

TerraMai
terramai.com
Producers of flooring, beams, paneling, and other products from wood reclaimed from a variety of sources, including old buildings and bridges, railroad ties, and abandoned logging operations.

Trestlewood
trestlewood.com
Dealers in reclaimed wood planks and beams.

Vermont Natural Coatings
vermontnaturalcoatings.com
Manufacturer of PolyWhey, a naturally derived wood finish made from the byproduct of cheesemaking that has the durability of an oil-based finish.

Vermont Soapstone
vermontsoapstone
Legendary miners of soapstone and makers of countertops, sinks, and more.

Vetrazzo
vetrazzo.com
Manufacturers of terrazzo-like surfacing that is 85% glass, 100% of which is recycled.

Waterworks
waterworks.com
Known for its high-end classic and designer plumbing fixtures and fittings, as well as bath furniture and accessories, many of which are handmade in Normandy, France.

Wicanders
wicanders.com
Makers of cork flooring since 1868.

WilsonArt
wilsonart.com
Manufacturer and distributor of high-pressure laminates used for countertops and flooring. With a wide array of patterns, they are now available in a custom option that allows you to turn any digital image into a surface material.

The Woods Company
thewoodscompany.com
Manufacturers of flooring from antique wood.

Yolo Colorhouse
yolocolorhouse.com
Creators of high-quality, zero-VOC paint.

Credits

We would like to thank the designers, architects, and builders who contributed to this book, and the homeowners who graciously allowed us to photograph their kitchens.

Photography

Abode/Beateworks/Corbis: 39 top left, 156 bottom right, 160 bottom left; K. Ahm/HofP/Inside/Photozest: 37 bottom left; courtesy of Alkemi: 62 bottom; Lucas Allen/GMAImages: 69 top, 149; Jean Allsopp: 150; APCOR: 130 left; Noam Armonn/Spaces Images/Corbis: 87 bottom right; Devis Bionas/GAP Interiors: 22 bottom; Botanica/Jupiterimages: 168 right; Marion Brenner: 33 bottom, 45 bottom; Todd Caverly: 160 bottom right; D. Chatz/H&L/Inside/Photozest: 187; Bieke Claessens/GAP Interiors: 222–223; John Clark: 35 top; Côté Sud/Nicolas Mathéus/GMAImages: 22 top right, 36, 193 right; courtesy of Dacor: 112 top left; Carrie Dodson Davis: 47 bottom middle; Dan Duchars/GAP Interiors: 129 top right, 219; courtesy of DuPont: 66 bottom right; courtesy of Eco Timber: 130 right, 134 top; Pieter Estersohn: 136–137 (all), 139 both; Pieter Estersohn/Beateworks/Corbis: 43 right; Shannon Fagan/Spaces Images/Corbis: 87 top; Elizabeth Felicella/Beateworks/Corbis: 38, 71; Marc Gerritsen/Lived In Images/Corbis: 189 top; Douglas Gibb/GAP Interiors: 27, 41; Tria Giovan: 56, 60 top right, 72–73, 75 (all), 91 bottom right, 131 left, 156 top, 178–179, 180–181 (all), 196–197, 198 bottom right, 199, 204–205 (all), 213; Tria Giovan/GAP Interiors: Front cover, 31, 43 top left, 191 top, back cover middle; John Granen: 44, 52–53 (all), 140–141 (all), 142–143 (all), 153, 154, 211; M. Green/H&L/Inside/Photozest: 164 bottom left; Ken Gutmaker: 160 top left;

Margot Hartford: 110 right, 127 bottom right, 163 top left, 163 bottom right, 164 top left; Tom Haynes: 135 bottom left, 135 bottom right; Eric Hernandez/Lived In Images/Corbis: 104; Maree Homer/ACP/Trunk Archive: 133 top right; House & Leisure/GMAImages: 3 middle, 3 right, 183, 207, 215; Rodney Hyet/Elizabeth Whiting & Associates/Corbis: 60 bottom; courtesy of IceStone: 62 middle; Bjarni B. Jacobsen/Pure Public/Living Inside: 186 top; Richard Leo Johnson/Beateworks/Corbis: 21 left; Rob Karosis: 111 left; courtesy of KitchenAid: 115 top; Raimund Koch/GMAimages: 57 top; M. Lanning/H&L/Inside/Photozest: 47 top left; Åke E:son Lindman/GMAImages: 60 top left, 126; Lived In Images/Corbis: 109 top; David Duncan Livingston: 32, 37 bottom right, 46, 59 middle, 61 top, 61 middle, 71 top left, 76–77 (all), 78–79 (all), 91 bottom left, 107 left, 112 top right, 112 bottom, 152 top right, 169 right, back cover top; Benjamin Mamet/GAP Interiors: 133 top left; Charles Maraia/The Image Bank/Getty Images: 127 left; Ellen McDermott: 10, 33 top, 59 bottom, 65, 70 top, 89 top, 109 middle, 109 bottom, 129 bottom, 151 left, 156 bottom left, 188; Matthew Millman: 48–51, 96, 97 top; Laura Moss/Country Living: 88; courtesy of PaperStone: 62 top; courtesy of Pergo: 128; Photoshot/Red Cover/Grey Crawford: 110 left; Photoshot/Red Cover/Jake Fitzjones: 61 bottom right; Photoshot/Red Cover/Winifried Heinze: 132; Photoshot/Red Cover/Paul Massey: 47 right; Photoshot/Red Cover/N. Minh & J. Wass: 89 bottom middle; Photoshot/Red Cover/Trine Thorsen: 61 bottom left, 189 bottom; Photoshot/Red Cover/Chris Tubbs: 18–19; Photoshot/Red Cover/Deborah Whitlaw-Llewellyn: 212; Costas Picadas/GAP Interiors: 42, 63; Richard Powers: 3 left, 125; Pro-Image Photography/Ed Sozinho:

4 top right; Paul Rivera/courtesy of Lacina Heitler Architects: 86–87; Lisa Romerein: 14 left, 14–15, 43 bottom left, 67, 131 right; M. Roobaert/Inside/Photozest: 66 top, 168 left; Jonathan Ross/Spaces Images/Corbis: 91 top; Eric Roth: 5 bottom left, 11, 22 top left, 25 bottom, 37 top, 40 top, 47 bottom left, 64, 89 middle right, 90, 92–93, 94 top right, 94 middle, 94 bottom, 95, 102–103, 113, 133 bottom left, 134 left, 155 bottom, 159 top, 163 top right, 164 top right, 165, 200–201 (all); Alexandra Rowley: 2 right, 20, 39 bottom, 55, 69 bottom, 85, 111 right, 114, 134 bottom right, 157, 164 bottom right, 167 top, 190, 192 (both); Jeremy Samuelson/FoodPix/Jupiterimages: 87 bottom left; Annie Schlechter: 59 top, 107 right, 115 bottom; Annie Schlechter/GMAImages: 21 right, 108, 185; Nick Scott/ACP/Trunk Archive: 195; Tom Scott/Red Cover/Getty Images: 162; Tom Sibley/Corbis: 16, 191 bottom; Michael Skott: 127 top right; Jacob Snavely/GMAImages: 35 bottom; Thomas J. Story: 9, 12, 13 top, 26, 47 top middle, 58, 71 top right, 89 middle left, 103 right, 151 right, 152 bottom left, 163 bottom left, 166, 174–175 (all), 176–177 (all), 193 left, 210–211; Tim Street-Porter: 24–25, 89 bottom right, 167 bottom; Robin Stubbart/GAP Interiors: 8; Amanda Turner/GAP Interiors: 186 bottom; Simon Upton/The Interior Archive: 194 top; Wouter Vandertol/GMAImages: 208–209; Dominique Vorillon: Front flap, 18 top, 18 bottom, 23, 25 top, 34, 39 top right, 45 top, 57 bottom, 66 left, 70 bottom, 106 left, 133 bottom right, 135 top, 152 bottom right, 160 top right, 184, 194, 198, 202–203 (all), back cover bottom; David Wakely: 152 top left; Julian Wass: 2 left, 7, 68, 89 bottom left, 101, 106 right, 155 top, 158, 159 bottom, 185 top, 216; Michelle Lee Wilson: 40 bottom, 80–81 (all), 82–83 (all), 97 bottom, 98–99 (all), 116–117 (all), 118 top right, 118

bottom right, 119, 120–121, 122–123 (all), 129 top left, 144–145 (all), 146–147 (all), 156 middle left, 161, 169 left, 170–171 (all), 172–173 (all); Polly Wreford: 1

Design

Front flap: Kathryn Ireland; 2 left: de Giulio Kitchen Design; 2 right: Olga Naiman and Jennifer Berno; 3 left: Georgie Bean (producer), Eckersley Garden Architecture (design); 7: de Giulio Kitchen Design; 11: Sebastian Carpenter Design; 12–13: Lara C. Dutto, D-Cubed; 14–15: Lewis/Schoeplein Architects; 18 top: Kenneth Brown; 18 bottom: Kerry Joyce; 20: Olga Naiman and Jennifer Berno; 22 top left: Heather G Wells Interiors; 22 top right: Laurence Dougier; 23: David Montalba, Montalba Architects; 25 top: David Michael Miller; 26: Susan Delurgio and Alisha Peterson, Beach House Style; 33 top: Stephen St. Onge; 34: Alexandra Champalimaud; 35 top: Sagan Piechota Architecture; 36: Laurence Dougier; 39 top right: Lynn Pries; 39 bottom: Olga Naiman and Jennifer Berno; 40 top: Niemtz Design Group (architects), Icon Group (interior design); 40 bottom: Holly Durocher for Reclaim Home + Design; 43 bottom left: Architecture by Frank Gehry, interior design by Michael Lee and homeowners Sue and Alex Glasscock; 44: Kevin Price and Kim Clements, JAS Design Build; 45 top: Doug Marsceill; 47 top middle: Lara C. Dutto, D-Cubed; 47 bottom left: Dalia Kitchen Designs; 48–51: Neal Schwartz, Schwartz and Architecture; 52–53: Kevin Price and Kim Clements, JAS Design Build; 55: Olga Naiman and Jennifer Berno; 56: David H. Mitchell Design; 57 top: Dolce & Burnham; 57 bottom: Madeline Stuart; 58: Francesca Quagliata, 4th Street Design; 59 bottom: Kimberlee Hansen; 60 top right: Heather Chadduck; 64: Heather G Wells Interiors; 66 left: Jeffrey

Illustration

Index

Sunset guides you to a fabulous home—inside and out

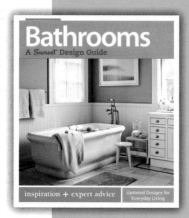

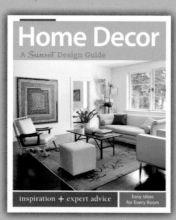